My Father, *this* side of Heaven

Table of Contents

My Father, *this* side of Heaven

Copyright 2012 by Gregory A. Hill

Published in the United States by

Gregory Anthony Hill Publishing Co.

Houston, Texas

Edited by

Catherine Ashley-Nelson

Printed in the United States

Book Cover Design by

Gregory A. Hill

My Father, *this* side of Heaven…

Acknowledgements

Although the people and events that provided the foundation of this book go back for over 30 years, the ideas that sparked it into reality come from a very recent past.

Organizations within the religious community as well as the secular community provided me many mentoring opportunities with young juvenile offenders. It is their plight that is the catalyst for this writing.

Since one of the main focuses of this book is mentoring, there is a special person I want to thank in that regard. Though we met as young adults, Ollie Patterson has not only been a mentor to me, but more than that, he's been a true friend. His support and advice helped to keep me stable when the ground beneath my feet sometimes rumbled.

Also to my dear sister Linda Vaughn, who provided inspiration, guidance, advice, and critical technical support for this work. This book could not have come to be had it not been for the combined efforts of all involved.

Prologue

And he will turn the hearts of the fathers to the children, and the hearts of the children to their fathers, lest I come and strike the earth with a curse.   Malachi 4:6

Who am I? Oh, I have an actual name that people use when they refer to me or need me for something. It simply tells others that I exist. But the real me, my history, purpose, attitude, and life destination is tied to my father. In order to know who I really am, I need to know him. I have read that when I get to heaven, God will give me a new name, a name that is known only to Him and me.

It will represent a relationship that is unique to us, a relationship that is different from everyone else's. That name will be the cornerstone of who and what I will be for all eternity. Although my life on this side of heaven will be considerably shorter, that unique relationship with my earthly father is also the cornerstone of this life's destiny. With my cornerstone missing, my history is incomplete, my purpose unsure, my attitude troubled, my destiny without direction, and my real name, unknown.

Introduction

Shortly after finishing college and moving to Texas, I took the opportunity to mentor young men in various places and organizations. From runaway shelters to juvenile facilities, I have accumulated nearly fifteen years of experience in the area of mentoring at the time of this writing. This venture has taken me from kids who have never been in trouble, to those who have run away from home, to those who have found themselves entangled in our juvenile justice system. Those experiences, along with many that simply come from living, paying attention, and raising my own sons, make up the foundation of what you are about to read.

For anyone who cares to look, it is plain to see that the male youth in the minority communities are in serious trouble. Fewer of these young men are going to college, while more and more of them are hanging on street corners, doing drugs, gang-banging, and going to jail. The number of young black men that are incarcerated has reached epidemic proportions.

While we all know that most social issues are typically complex, there is almost always one element of any issue that can be called a main ingredient, and usually everything else revolves around it. This book looks to highlight and examine the catastrophic dynamics of absentee fathers in America, particularly how it relates to juvenile incarceration.

In looking at this situation, my initial conclusion was probably about the same as it was, or is, for some of you. These kids knew that their criminal behavior was wrong, and I am confident that they knew the likely consequences of their actions. I even expect that many of them have seen at least one episode of the series "Scared Straight". Also, many of these young men are already on their second and third arrest. Certainly there are other kids from similar circumstances that chose not to run afoul of the law. Perhaps these kids are only getting what they deserve. Those who chose criminal activity just decided to be bad apples.

With that being said, my personal observation has led me to conclude that more than ninety-percent of the males in prison are ones that come from homes without a father, or where the father-son relationship is severely strained. The absence of good, strong fathers, (or sometimes the presence of a terrible one), plays a powerful and significant role in a boy's life. It goes without saying that the absence of fathers is due to a number of reasons, with plenty of blame to go around for both parents. It leads to a large number of emotional and psychological pitfalls, which usually results in making bad decisions. These pitfalls leave these young boys frustrated, confused, angry, and sad. They tear down the necessary building blocks that are needed for identity, discipline, direction, and purpose in life. Many times these pitfalls turn out to be criminal activities. It is virtually an undeniable fact that there is a direct connection between the out of control juvenile activity, and fatherless homes.

The extremely high percentage of minority teens in our juvenile systems set off an alarm in my head. Since I have worked primarily with African-American males, they will be the focus of this book. Although the Hispanic and African-American communities are most affected, the emotional and social destruction resulting from fatherless homes has no ethnic or racial boundaries. I am fully convinced that our young girls are being negatively affected also, but in a slightly different way. So, much of what is contained here can be applied to our young daughters as well.

Households led by both mother and father should be at the top of everyone's endangered species list. A clear reminder of this crisis comes to mind when I think of a statement made by my one of my younger relatives. The discussion led to someone mentioning that my immediate family of eleven siblings was the result of the same mother and father. In her amazement she replied, "Wow, that's unbelievable! To my knowledge, none of my friends have siblings with the same mother and father"!

In communities across this country, the number of African-American children today coming from single parent homes is constantly on the rise, and in some places are as high as eighty percent. I think it goes without saying that the single parent is almost always the mother.

In 1972, Gladys Knight and the Pips recorded a song that probably broadcasts the message of this book louder than any number of pages I can write. For those of you who are old enough to remember, the song title is, "This child needs his Father". Near the end of the song, this is the mother's lament; *"he calls for daddy every day, and you're not there. I'm running out of things to say, how can I tell him, that you just don't care?"*

I recognize that I am not the first person to acknowledge or write about the importance of the father-son relationship, and I hope I'm not the last. However, sometimes we need to be reminded of important things so that we don't forget or overlook them. Perhaps you have never realized that so many of our young men are being arrested and detained each day. If so, you are ahead of the game. If not, perhaps this will serve as a wake-up call.

My Father, *this* side of Heaven

Dedication

Virtually throughout the history of African-Americans in the United States, mothers have been the heart and soul of our families and communities. Much has been said and written concerning the incredible strength, dedication, and determination of African-American mothers in terms of their part in holding their families together. The poem below, by Elizabeth A. Robinson, is just one expression of such.

You Are My Heart and Soul

Thank you...
For standing by me through thick and thin
For not giving up on me when I didn't win
For your patience when I kept pushing you away
For caring when I said I didn't need you anyway
I am grateful knowing...
I can count on your strength
Ask for your support, and know you'll go to any length
When I lose my way
You help me get back on track
When in pain
Your comfort soothes and brings me back
I am lucky because...
When I was sad you gave me faith and hope
When I was confused you taught me how to cope

My Father, *this* side of Heaven

When I felt I couldn't go on
You carried me long miles
When I didn't believe
You restored my smiles
Mom, Thank you
For your guidance and you faith you've shown
For giving me a safe place where I have grown
For showing me how to strive
Because of your love
I will survive...

This book is dedicated to those young men who have managed to fight and overcome the wrong temptations and challenges of growing up without their fathers, and have turned what was a lack into a pursuit of purpose, success and dignity. And, secondly, to the ones who have taken the wrong road but managed to turn their ship around and get back on the path to a productive and meaningful life. Thirdly, to the strong and determined single mothers who have met the challenge, despite tremendous odds, and managed to raise their sons to be strong, responsible, successful young men who are a credit to their family, community, and society.

Chapter 1

Where we Are

While statistics don't tell the entire story, some are virtually impossible to argue with. Be that as it may, these statistics argue for themselves: According to the website www.innocentdads.org:

1) 43% of US children live without their father [US Department of Census]

2) 90% of homeless and runaway children are from fatherless homes. [US D.H.H.S., Bureau of the Census]

3) 80% of rapists motivated with displaced anger come from fatherless homes.

[Criminal Justice & Behaviour, Vol 14, pp. 403-26, 1978]

4) 71% of pregnant teenagers lack a father. [U.S. Department of Health and Human Services press release, Friday, March 26, 1999]

5) 63% of youth suicides are from fatherless homes. [US D.H.H.S., Bureau of the Census]

6) 85% of children who exhibit behavioral disorders come from fatherless homes. [Center for Disease Control]

7) 90% of adolescent repeat arsonists live with only their mother. [Wray Herbert, "Dousing the Kindlers," Psychology Today, January, 1985, p. 28]

8) 71% of high school dropouts come from fatherless homes. [National Principals Association Report on the State of High Schools]

9) 75% of adolescent patients in chemical abuse centers come from fatherless homes. [Rainbows f for all God's Children]

10) 70% of juveniles in state operated institutions have no father. [US Department of Justice, Special Report, Sept. 1988]

11) 85% of youths in prisons grew up in a fatherless home. [Fulton County Georgia jail populations, Texas Department of Corrections, 1992]

From my experience of multiple visits to the juvenile facilities in Harris County, Texas from 2008 - 2012, I can tell you that upwards of 75% of the incarcerated youth in Harris County, Texas are from the black and Hispanic communities. That falls in line with the statistics from the National Kids count Program website. Their research established that in states where there is any significant minority population, the blacks and Hispanics had nearly three times the number of single parent households.

In today's society we find ourselves far removed from many of the traditional norms and values that made us strong in times past. Over the last several decades the welfare of the family, community and country has been replaced with welfare of "me". Our norms and values were once rooted in a strong sense of integrity, coming largely as a natural result of a life lived with respect for God and man. Pushing aside those values has laid the groundwork for the rising numbers of divorces, child abandonments, out-of wedlock pregnancies, and various other social problems. Obviously this has been a major player in producing an abundance of single-parent homes.

A change of direction is truly necessary if the African-American community is going to survive. Therefore, this book may well be described as an attempt to introduce a type of paradigm shift. A paradigm (pair-a-dime) shift is a radical change in the way something is done or thought of. It means looking at situations and ideas just the opposite of how they were previously viewed. It is a term that is most commonly used in business circles. It attempts to bring in a new look at an old belief or concept.

Paradigm shifts rarely go over well. They are usually met with furious anger, hostility, and sometimes violence. They go against our sacred traditions, comforts and conveniences.

******

One notable example that I heard of was the introduction of the digital watch. Before the technology was available, the mindset was that a watch always had to have hands on a dial. When someone introduced the idea of LED digits replacing the traditional watch face, some watchmakers resisted the idea. Most believed the idea would fail. That inability to accept the new idea caused them to lose a considerable share of the watch marketplace.

******

First, we must re-evaluate the role and significance of fathers. The priceless value of what fathers contribute to children, especially the boys, must be seen for its true value. Secondly, we must come back to a realization of the importance of a two-parent household. If we don't change the way we think about the "new normal" single-family structure, the price we will continue to pay will be more lives and futures lost that can't be valued in money. A move back in the direction towards the two-parent family is an absolute must. Thirdly, traditional family court ideology needs some adjustment. Too often the amount of time fathers are allowed to spend with their children is not nearly enough. That is particularly important when it comes to pre-teen boys.

Chapter 2
The Perfect Storm

In sailing the open seas, perhaps the most feared and deadly event is called the perfect storm. It is a rare combination of several weather patterns happening at the same time that create massive storms. They produce extremely strong winds, heavy rain, and huge ocean waves that few ships or sailors have ever survived. Unfortunately, for many of our young men, a "social" perfect storm is a way of life and few are surviving. They are bombarded daily with its harsh elements.

To begin with, the importance of God in our homes and communities that once blew as a mighty wind has been downgraded to a faint summer breeze. Instead, our society has chosen to sail in seas with hurricane force winds that serve up vulgar, degrading music, movies, and x-rated TV and internet videos. The media's embracing of prison and gang culture is being swallowed up by our young men and women like fast food. This is partly to blame for the unashamed use of vulgar language in the presence of elders. In past generations it was a rare occurrence. It is now commonplace.

Another element of this storm is the heavy rains of abandonment and betrayal by parents. Those rains wash away a child's foundation of faith. When faith in parents is damaged, it is leads to children having less faith in society as a whole. Consequently, children are robbed of a critical building block of their character. It leads children to seek out gangs and other unhealthy groups or activities in order to try and replace that missing foundation.

Thirdly, the ominous number 13: As we all know, the number 13 has been the center of much superstition for centuries. Those superstitions range from Friday the 13th, to not labeling building floors or airline aisles with that number, and on and on. Oddly enough, when it comes to predicting when the storm in a boy's life will occur, age 13 keeps popping up. You can almost set your watch by it.

When these young men reach their early teen years and the realities of their situations come into focus, the picture they see is a painful one. That is usually when the anguish, disappointment, and frustration of a broken family sets in and gets acted out. Amazingly, virtually every troubled young man I have encountered or asked about had their troubling behavior begin at about that age. Some of these young men have had several arrests by the age of 15.

The pain and disillusionment that lingers from an abusive and un-loving father is devastating. It is surpassed only by the feeling of betrayal and abandonment of a father that simply doesn't want to be one, and isn't there. Once tossed overboard without the support from the father, the attempt to swim ashore against the powerful waves of life is too difficult for many to manage alone.

Though the details of each life are as different as are the children that live them, the factors that result in the downfall of these young men are nearly as predictable as the rising sun. In the generation following the civil rights movement, the progress of African-American men was seemingly moving in a positive direction. An unfortunate reversal has quickly taken shape. More and more of our sons are washing up on the shores of life with no direction. They are wandering aimlessly through life, from street corner to street corner. They have little desire for education, and too many are rapidly filling the halls of our criminal justice system. There seems to be no end in sight.

Chapter 3

Do We REALLY Need Dads?

When one of my sons was in middle school, he came home one day with a sobering story. In talking to one of his female classmates, she shared with him her promise that though one day she may get married, she vowed that she would never have children. When he asked why, she told him that her father abandoned her and her younger brother. After describing the agony her little brother went through because of dad's departure, she said she could not bear the thought of having her son's father leave, and watch her own son endure that kind of suffering.

******

I recently reconnected with someone I had briefly dated in college. As she talked about her life after divorce and raising her son alone, she quickly offered her thoughts on the subject. Her emotional outburst went something like this: "If I could climb to the highest place on earth and scream at the top of my lungs, my cry to the whole world would be, "BOYS NEED THEIR DADS!"

A healthy family structure needs both parents. The simple truth is that both mother and father play a key role in raising an emotionally healthy child. Each parent brings traits to the child emotionally and psychologically that is unique to their gender. Raising healthy children requires balance. As in preparing a meal, if a recipe calls for salt and pepper, leaving either one out makes it extremely difficult to end up with a tasteful dish.

The importance of the father's presence has been severely misunderstood and grossly undervalued in our society. When children are born out of wedlock, the chances of the father being absent are obviously higher than when the parents had been married. Furthermore, even an "involved" absentee father often cannot have the impact that is needed because he is doing it part time, and/or from a distance.

******

I had a discussion about this subject with a long-time friend who had a child out of wedlock.   He cared for his son, (who lived across town with his mother), fulfilled his financial commitment, and was heavily involved in his son's life. Nevertheless, the son still managed to stray into criminal activity. Since the father put so much time into his son's life, he felt that absentee fathers were not a significant factor in children's behavior. He cited that the real problem is that children spend too much time being lazy and are not kept busy doing something meaningful. In an indirect way, he made my point. Often the main reason that children are allowed to be lazy and non-productive is that there are no fathers *in* the home to manage and discipline them!

******

The relationship that connects a father and a son carries more power and importance than past society has recognized. I believe it is a spiritual connection that provides the foundation for identity, strength, love, self-esteem, faith and purpose in a young boy's life. If a son is raised only by his father, he will definitely be missing an important part of what mom brings to the table. Either way, a child from a single parent family will typically have a tougher mountain to climb.

Out of curiosity, I conducted a small survey of my own. I posed a situation to several mothers, and every one of them has agreed with me on this. Here it is: in most cases, it is more difficult for most boys to deal with the effects of an absentee father than it is to deal with the effects of an absentee mother.

Far too many times, a mother's love and nurturing just isn't enough. A mother's attempt to fill the father's role is like trying to fit a square peg into a round hole. Neither our communities nor our society will survive without the adequate presence of decent fathers in the home.

There are some who want to convince society that having both mother and father to raise a child is not important. More and more we see same sex couples adopting and "having" children, trying to support that belief. While the subject of same sex couples is not my main subject matter here, I must address this issue. It is not my purpose or intent to bash or put down how those couples decide to live their lives. However, to even begin to assert that they can raise emotionally healthy children with complete disregard for gender is another matter.

There are even some special interest groups who are pushing an effort to remove all gender identity from society, making everything "normal", and giving license to every ideology that makes *them* comfortable. The unfortunate hatred and intolerance toward people whom society has improperly oppressed, shunned, belittled, and ostracized, has fueled a movement for their survival. The quest is on to ignore and defy nature and God in order to find a place of acceptance and equality in society. While the quest to be treated as people is legitimate, I have no doubt that attempts to discount the need for dual sexuality is misguided and destructive to society.

Some of the most important things we learn from our parents don't come from lectures or preaching. They come by example. The motto of the mentoring organization '100 Black Men' is, *"what they see is what they will be"*. Particularly when it comes to character issues, children are much more likely to do what you do, rather than what you say. A former pastor of mine expressed the psychology this way, "What you do speaks so loudly, I can't hear what you say".

Nearly every son, at least in the early stages of life, aspires to be just like dad. If dad is not around to look to, their guidance system lacks part of what it needs in order to function properly. Often they must look sideways to their peers, or mom, for "manly" direction, validation and acceptance. Now, to some degree, looking for a level of validation from one's peers is quite normal. However, when experiencing the emotional effects of an absentee (or dysfunctional) father, the peers that are available often are an unhealthy source. Destructive behavior is just around the corner.

When we are born into this world our mind is virtually blank and the natural thing for us to do is to identify ourselves with our primary caretaker(s). As we grow older and learn our names and familiarize ourselves with our surroundings, our profile of who we are begins to take shape. This profile tells us where we fit in our family, community and society. It helps set the standards for how we process the other influences we receive. The father/son relationship is a critical piece of who we usually become, good or bad. This cornerstone of our "building" determines the reference point upon which we build our lives.

If we adore, respect, and look up to our fathers, it is natural to want to be like him in the way he functions in life.   This universal connection is one where a son identifies with a man he is proud of, holding him in the highest esteem. With that comes the assumption that he is loved and accepted unconditionally. No father is, or has to be perfect. If he can simply get a passing grade in the love and acceptance areas toward his son, it would be a solid building block to start from.

Along with the lack of fathers present in the home, the other most common element is the problem of the company boys tend to keep. They have a need to run with the boys on the block. They have to be a part of the crowd. Most of the boys I have dealt with probably would never have gotten into trouble if they associated with different groups, or just were by themselves. Most parents constantly tell their sons "don't hang around with those boys; they are going to get you into trouble". While those are words are spoken loud and clear, they are often ignored. That message is much more difficult to ignore if it comes from a strong but loving father.

The desire and need for group acceptance is a normal part of life. It is perhaps at its peak in adolescence. Again, a major part of our identity is tied to our family and to the father in particular. That identity is supposed to be rooted in an unconditional love and acceptance. Since that emotional need is so great, boys will stretch the boundaries of their activity to dangerous and unhealthy limits to get it. As a part of their masculine nature, immaturity, and emotional turmoil, criminal behavior often becomes irresistible bait. Studies have all but proven that the immediate community where a child grows up can be a stronger influence than the home itself!

When a broken, fatherless home is added to bad community influences, it increases the chances of these young men leaning toward crime. One of the major factors causing minority communities to be such a negative influence is the fact that there are not enough fathers *in* the community! It is a vicious cycle that feeds on itself.

******

Kendall, one of my mentees, told me that throughout his earlier life, his big brother was mostly away and his mom was always at work. He was constantly being harassed and beaten up, in addition to spending much too much time alone. Even though his mother loved him, her personal and financial struggles made it difficult to recognize that her son was drowning in loneliness and fear. She wouldn't let him on the football team, fearing for his safety, not to mention there was really not time for such things. He felt isolated and his value system was eroding. Along comes the gang, providing him the fellowship of friends, protection, respect, and validation. During my second visit with him he told me that in his mind, the gang was the best thing that ever happened to him, and that he vowed to be a life-long member. At his young age, and from his limited perspective, negative, gang-related activity was a small price to pay for the benefits of his new value system. By the end of his third year of incarceration, his perspective had begun to change.

******

Justin, another mentee who was 15 when I met him, was trying to deal with a lingering tragedy. While in grade school his father shot and killed his mother (virtually in front of him), and then proceeded to take his own life. I don't think I need to say any more about what happened to his direction and identity. As of this writing, he is still trying to maneuver his way through the penal system, and recovery is still ongoing.

******

The value of good parental relationships can't be measured in a lab or probed by an MRI. Single parents wage a huge battle trying to play two roles. Most attempts from fathers to impart things that are natural and instinctive to mothers are like trying to pass off canned biscuits for homemade ones. If you are from the south as I am, you know it falls short. Yes, those canned biscuits did meet the need in curing my hunger. They also supplied some nutrition, but they simply were not the same as the homemade ones.

A former pastor of mine once made a statement that really rings true. He said that in this modern age we have so many artificial things we eat, that often the artificial becomes more desirable than the real thing. Most artificial things involve shortcuts, usually leaving out ingredients that outwardly seem to be of little value. However, in the long run it usually costs more in the end. For boys to be properly nourished emotionally they need proper father figures. Most of the other substitutes are usually a recipe for disaster.

******

In 2011, sports writer Jason Whitlock posted an internet video that featured a panel discussion about black athletes who were raised without a father. One topic centered on the question of why there are decreasing numbers of young black men playing baseball.

One of the panelists, Hall of Fame football player Michael Irvin, gave his input. He said that when he grew up only a few kids in the area had fathers at home. He noted that he and his friends realized that no father was around to help build their identity as men. Therefore, they began to look to one another for that "anointing." Since playing football or basketball made you look tough and manly in the eyes of your peers, it became a tool many used to validate themselves as a man. In the eyes of his peers, baseball was considered a sport for chumps, so it was shunned. Michael's bottom line opinion was this;

"Only a man, by his example, can teach you to be a man. Try as she might, mama can't do it".

******

When parents are not together, distance becomes a problem for adequate two-parent involvement. In many cases, each parent chooses to fulfill their dream of how and where they want to live. In almost every case, it is the children who pay the heaviest price. That price is some level of emotional trauma. This not meant to be an indictment of every parent that finds themselves in that situation. Nevertheless, I believe too many parents make decisions with the attitude that *their* life and happiness is more important than the child's emotional well-being. Even worse, many times the parent's attitude is, "well, that's life, they'll just have to deal with it". I wonder what would happen if the powers were reversed and the children could force the parents to stay together and "just deal with it"? Interesting idea.

Please know that it is not my intent to judge anyone who is divorced, for I too, am one of you. I will be the first to acknowledge that divorce is something we will always deal with in this imperfect world. They happen among all racial, ethnic, and religious groups. With that being said, I sometimes wonder how much harder we all would try if we could *really* see what it does to our children.

******

When I met Jay he was a seventeen year old on probation for aggravated robbery and several probation violations. He had been raised by a single mom who had a difficult and troubled childhood. In trying to balance work and single-parenting, she was unable to give Jay the attention he felt he needed. Around the age of 13 he found himself on the road to trouble. It started in school, acting out and acting up. With no father around frustrations mounted for both. It wasn't long before Jay was kicked out of the house and criminal mischief quickly turned to criminal behavior. In one of our sessions, I asked him about his mindset that allowed him to engage in some serious criminal behavior. My question was, "weren't you afraid of getting caught and going to jail?" His reply was simple, "at the time I was so angry and frustrated I didn't care". When I asked about the mindset of some of the other guys he met while locked up, he gave me some sobering insight. Some of the teens were hoping to get locked up! Outside of jail they had nowhere to go and no one who cared about their well-being. At least in prison they had structure, a place to sleep, and food to eat.

Chapter 4

System Failure

The proper relationship we have with our parents is the foundation of the value system that we all need. It is a two-part system with the physical needs being food, clothing, shelter, and the physical presence of parents. The second part is emotional, being the need for love, faith, identity, and acceptance. These provide the very essential elements that children need to build a sense of personal security that is vital to a quality life.

Faith

The strongest and most important element in our existence is faith. For many of you this may sound ludicrous but if you think about it objectively you have no choice but to agree. Virtually all major decisions that will affect your life are based on faith. Just to clarify, faith simply is a belief in something as a result of encountering and experiencing enough **evidence**, sometimes with little or no scientific or factual data. For example, when a person decides to get married, get on an airplane, take medicine, make decisions as a juror, or even eat at a restaurant, those are all examples of exercising faith. Harmful and sometimes deadly results can arise from improper decisions in any of those situations. You have no concrete facts (or don't bother to get them) to support your decisions. Therefore your actions are simply based on faith, in someone or something.

As a newborn baby, you are totally dependent upon your caretaker for survival. As you grow older and are being properly taken care of, you naturally develop faith in that caretaker to feed and clothe you. This evidence forms the basis of your faith- the history of the relationship. When that is done, a natural love develops as a result of that faith. That primary, fundamental value system element of faith has been developed. It is the cornerstone of the remaining elements in the system.

The destruction of that faith opens the door for a new value system causing a skewed perspective of life and reality which leads to making bad decisions. Those decisions are reflected in bad personal habits and choices concerning education, marriage, finances, and a host of other day-to-day actions. These usually range from irresponsible sexual activity to running afoul of the law.

Love

The need to feel loved and needed is as important to emotional survival as food is to physical survival. In fact, it may be more so. We all know that the prolonged absence of food will lead to physical death. I also believe that the prolonged absence of love can also lead to physical death. In some ways that may be longer and more painful! Studies have shown that if a newborn baby goes too long without ever being physically touched it can actually die! In the absence of true love, our new value system will find a substitute. When you are in desperate need for physical food your brain will adjust your value system in order to validate your actions. The same principle applies when it comes to needing love. The most common and readily available substitute is sexual activity.

Identity

Who am I? That was the first question presented as you opened this book. Our own concept of who we are is another critical part of our emotional and psychological makeup. It may be because it starts the moment we are born. Though it may change, it is at the root of everything we are for the rest of our lives. It builds a sense of significance and tells us that we are important. If that significance doesn't come from its intended source of father and family, the next place to look to is the outside community. Often the destructive elements are the most attractive, and right outside the door.

Imagine that you have just awakened from a very long sleep. You quickly realized something was very wrong, but you weren't sure what. At that moment, in walks a doctor and informs you that you were in a terrible accident and suffered brain damage. As a result, you suffered a form of amnesia, and you cannot remember anyone from your past! You were told that you were 13 years old. You recognize no one.   Although physically you are okay, you don't even know your own name. It is as if you have just been born. The main question in your head is, "Who am I"?

We need something or someone as a support system. Those things typically come from whomever we identify with. So at 13 here we are, back at square one looking for security, purpose, respect, self-esteem, and love. Not only is it important how you see yourself, but more so how you think others see you.

When reality leads a teen to realize that a vital part or parts of his value system is missing, the search is on. Gang life is often on the next corner. To start, there is strength and power in numbers. With that comes a certain amount of control and support. Now let's add in something that looks good and brings respect in the eyes of others. Next, how can I reverse these unhappy circumstances, and get quick money to buy the things it seems I could never before afford? Where can I release this adrenaline? What is out there that I *know* I can fit into?

Being a substitute, gang life is part reality, part illusion. It is partly an illusion because much of what is valued is artificial. Things such as love, respect and family are only shadows of the real thing. The tangible things such as money, girls, and power are more real. The personal security and control is more than existed before and completing the initiation brings immediate significance.

"Gang" respect is not true respect. In reality, if respect is simply based in fear it is false. True respect is built on character not fear. The commitment to the gang is based on unbendable rules and fear, not love. Only evil tyrants or insecure rulers control groups by force or fear. If true love were a bonding element, disobedience would not be met with violent or fatal consequences. Certainly as you spend time and activities with people a sense of family can develop. However, if one chooses to leave the family there should be sorrow, not fear.

Now, imagine you were born in England and your father was the king. Presto! From the day of your birth you have been a prince and everyone knows it. Once you get old enough to realize who you are, you have no need to prove yourself and your significance to anyone. Because of who your parents are, you don't need the approval of any of your peers, (they want yours), and there is no need to adjust your value system. Perhaps the most difficult message to get across to young men is this; you don't have to be a prince or have a prominent ancestry to have validation, just a father whom you can admire.

Acceptance

Acceptance is another part of what makes a person feel loved, especially in adolescence. That basic need to fit in and be a part of something is simply a part of our DNA. Apart from sound family relationships, some boys manage to find acceptance in team sports, band membership, R.O.T.C., or other associations.

For those who are not keen on sports or some other mainstream group, the gang element becomes attractive bait. In a gang, the benefits are immediate. In a short period of time the new gang member now has sense of power, protection, camaraderie, money, clothes, cars, women, respect, and, of course, acceptance. Teens, like some of us adults, rarely focus on the long term results of their actions, only the immediate rewards. It can very easily blind them to the full reality of the possible consequences, especially in the beginning.

This need for acceptance is further verified by the fact that many times the initiation process into the gang doesn't come easily. Consider that boys often endure extreme physical distress, or inflict that on someone else just to be included. That partially indicates how important it is to them at the time.

******

A former pastor of mine recalled a story about raising his teenage son. When the son turned twelve years old and was allowed to go to the park alone and "hang" with the neighborhood kids, he came home an hour later looking and acting like the other kids, (you know, pants sagging, hat on backwards, and a new way to speak the English language). The father's bewildering question was, "What did those kids do in one hour to change what I had instilled in him over the last twelve years?!

******

Two words, peer pressure. (It is not quite that simple, but almost).

When you talk to boys about their sagging pants, excessive tattoos or body piercings, it makes no difference to them how the practice started or what it meant at the time. All they care about is that it is something that helps them to fit in, giving them a sense of acceptance. I am reminded of a line in gospel artist Kirk Franklin's song, "Shout, Let it all Out". In reference to his teenage years of turmoil he states, "I wanted to be accepted so bad I was willing to die". In the minds of most teens today, that is not too far from the truth.

Even if the child is accepted and loved at home, there is still a need for a measure of acceptance outside of the home. That is where the immediate community comes in. Since all children must at some time venture outside, they will look for an additional feeling of acceptance in the neighborhood or school. A good value system at home helps children to make better choices outside of the home.

As a result, a large number of boys that fall into the category of what I would call "borderline criminals" take that next step because of the crowd they look to gain acceptance from. I hear it over and over- he's really not a bad kid, he just got hooked up with the wrong crowd. Most of the time, the juvenile has heard that warning over and over, but the desire for acceptance in the crowds proves to be too much to resist. It often requires the influence of mom, dad, relatives, friends and neighbors to save some boys from the lure of gangs. Most boys don't have anywhere near that much support.

Security

When we feel secure, there is little or no need to stretch our moral boundaries to seek false safety and comfort. When our value system or certain parts of it are destroyed, our primary objective becomes finding ways to replace the missing part(s).

A feeling of security is necessary in order to have a quality life. Children understand at an early age that their parents are supposed to be committed to each other and to them. Even when other parts of the value system are lacking, a strong foundation of love and commitment can be enough to make up the difference. That commitment is a major part of the foundation children need in order to feel secure.

As children mature their awareness grows of how their security is dependent upon the parents' commitment to the family. When families break up, shattering that commitment, trauma takes center stage. It often starts the search for a committed group outside of the home. Outside of mere survival, a lack of feeling secure can do far more damage than the physical deficiencies in a value system.

For all of the negative things that can be said for gangs there is a twisted irony that can't be denied. When people get married and state in their wedding vows, "'til death do us part", too often that promise is not kept. In gangs, they really mean it.

My Father, *this* side of Heaven

A few years ago, I was watching a documentary about an organization that was dedicated to finding all of our military's prisoners of war and those who went missing in action. The mindset that fueled the passion for their mission was this; "When men go off to war, they have accepted the fact that they may come home wounded. They have accepted the fact that they may even die in battle. Never do they expect to be abandoned". Abandonment is not supposed to be a part of the military value system. A child's perspective is the same.

******

One ten year old expressed his confusion and disappointment about his dad. He was able to somehow come to grips with the fact that his father had gotten into trouble and gone to prison for a short time. The son was able to deal with this feeling of temporary abandonment and resulting insecurity. The son's reasoning allowed him to conclude that his father had just made a once in lifetime mistake and life would soon return to normal.   After being released and back home, the father soon ran afoul of the law and was again incarcerated. After the second time the father was jailed, the son fell into a confused, bewildered state of mind. He was left to ponder how the father that he thought loved him would ever again do anything that would result in him going away again. The son's anguish, disappointment, and confusion provided fertile soil for a new value system to grow in.

******

One of the most incredible elements of our human makeup is the seemingly supernatural ability to adapt, particularly when it comes to survival. When we are confronted with physical or emotional survival our brains have the ability to take our mind and bodies into a survival mode. We all are vulnerable to move to things we once thought we would never do.

Replacing the basic value system sometimes leads to survival mode. If a person remains in survival mode too long, it can become a way of life. A survival value system is dangerous and sometimes deadly. That new system is an emotional paradigm shift, deemed necessary in order to survive. Gangs represent what appears to be a better value system. Remember that male validation Michael Irvin talked about? An important element of that new system starts with someone to look up to. Since there is no dad to look up to and get it from, boys look across to their peers and see what appears to be a good substitute.

The typical street gang has its own set of laws. The very first one is to never assist the law by being a witness.

The saying goes, "snitches get stitches and wind up in ditches". On the other hand, mainstream society at least attempts to follow a different policy. In an upright society citizens need to offer appropriate assistance in order to bring about justice for victims of crime. It is a vital part of maintaining a civil society. They would want that in return if they were the victim. Gang rules are just the opposite. This is a perfect example of how a necessary part of society's value system is turned upside down.

******

In the early 70's there were plane crash survivors who were lost in a snowy wilderness. Some survived in the snow by eating the bodies of the dead passengers in order to survive. While food is necessary for survival, humans in most cultures of the world would be horrified at the thought of eating human flesh. (Probably most, if not all, of those survivors would have never believed they were capable of such two months before). Though each of our personalities may be different, few of us truly know to what extent we will go to survive. How hungry and desperate would you have to get before you decided to eat out of a trash can, not caring who is looking? Be careful with saying "I'll never..."

When a person faces the desperation of street life often the only option that is realistic to them is to sell their bodies for food or drugs. That requires their brain to override their previous value system. The need for food or drugs moves to first place in their value system. Satisfying either is now more important than the risk of the extremely dangerous and demeaning behavior of prostitution. Until that hunger is satisfied, nothing else matters anyway.

******

At this point allow me to interject an idea that I believe often leads to unfair judgment against people in general, children in particular. Because we as humans are so guided by what we see, we often miss some underlying, unseen factors in people's behavior. It is quite obvious that we all have different strengths and weakness. When it comes to visual things such as intellect and athletic ability, it is clear that some of us are better with our hands, while some are better with their minds.

However, many of us seem to think that everyone is gifted with the same emotional and psychological strengths. It simply is not so! How many times have you "judged" a person's actions or heard someone else do it, by saying, "well I went through the same thing and I didn't react that way, so they didn't have to either." While that sometimes may be appropriate, that is certainly not equally true across the board for every person and every situation. Just as we have different physical and intellectual strengths and weaknesses, we also have different strengths and weaknesses when it comes to emotional things.

The scriptures even tell us, "Those who are strong should help out those who are weak." Those weaknesses include emotional and psychological areas. Again, this is not intended to be an excuse for all juvenile behavior, but rather to note that just as physically disabled people often need assistance, many of our emotionally disabled children need help, and a second chance.

******

Children discern early in life the difference between discipline and abuse, and where they should fit in the ladder of importance. Of all of the negative things that parents can inflict on their children, a sense that they are not really loved or wanted is almost always the toughest to deal with. Often, even in the face of abuse, children still defend their parent's actions, taking the blame for their parent's abusive behavior. In the mind and psyche of a child, an inherent belief in parents often allows children to excuse, justify, and take the blame for many of the parents' wrongdoings and abuses.

Frustration

As the confusion, fears, sense of loss and abandonment, unanswered questions, and a shattered value system comes to a head the end result is a mountain of frustration. When frustration has reached its boiling point a corresponding response is inevitable. Most crimes are the end result of frustration. It provides a resting place for all the hurt, disillusionment, disappointment, anger, and feelings of hopelessness. Given the natural, aggressive nature of most boys, criminal activity is as soothing to their emotional turmoil as aloe cream is to burning skin.

Lest we forget, even those of us who consider ourselves well-adjusted adults fall prey to the demon of frustration. How recent was the last time you retaliated at the driver that cut you off in traffic? What words have you said to your spouse or child out of frustration, that you wish you could take back? Frustration leads to more bad decisions and actions than probably any other emotion.

My parent's generation had to operate with a significant handicap when it came to child-rearing. Although I had what I considered to be good and loving parents, their background and upbringing created an inflexible boundary of acceptance, understanding, and tolerance. There was no understanding of the concept of dealing with eleven different children eleven different ways. I believe it can be summed up in this: W*e as parents have given all of you food, clothing, and shelter. We've taught you right from wrong-there is nothing else you need.*

They felt that since all were raised the same way, all should turn out the same way. I believe that inflexibility was partly to blame for some of my siblings living frustrated and unproductive lives. The socio-economic structure of my childhood served to help limit our perspective on life's possibilities, thereby making it difficult for some of us to find a place for our talents and dreams, helping to fuel frustrations. Unfortunately that situation is still much too widespread in minority communities.

When anyone, particularly, children, feel that there is no outlet to express themselves properly and be understood, frustration is at the doorstep. If frustration is not resolved, it will usually be acted out in negative or unproductive ways.

******

One of my brothers happened to be left handed and he stuttered. Being left handed was considered unhealthy and harmful in previous generations, so he was constantly being slapped on the hand each time he attempted to use it, hoping to discourage its use. It didn't work. He was constantly ridiculed for his stuttering. He spoke of other frustrations that may seem trivial to most of us but he had no outlet to calm them. We may never know if, or how big a part the handling of those elements were in creating or adding to his frustration, and his decision to reconstruct his value system toward a life of crime.

******

Galindo's Story-The Birth of a Mentor

(An article from The-Signal.com web page, posted February 3, 2011)

Efren Galindo isn't quite sure how he kept his family together. In September 1999, his father died of cancer. Four months later, his mother passed away from symptoms related to multiple sclerosis. At 19, Galindo had an enormous responsibility. East Newhall had rampant drug and gang problems then, and Galindo had to take on the role his father had with him: keeping his 17-year-old sister and 16-year-old brother out of trouble while managing two jobs and college courses. His experiences as a young man ushering young lives through East Newhall's rough years served as the foundation for his future career as sports coordinator at the Newhall Community Center. Through the position, Galindo mentors children and teenagers who are faced with challenges at home and struggling to stay out of trouble. He also walks the neighborhood with other city workers to make improvements, painting houses and planting grass. "You can't come to me and tell me I don't understand what it's like," he said.

Galindo relates Community center coordinator Julie Calderon said Galindo has earned respect from the kids who come to the center.

"He has very close ties with the teens," Calderon said. "He's a father figure and big brother at the same time. They can come up to him and talk to him about sensitive issues, and they know he's going to give them the best advice possible."
Growing up under difficult circumstances makes it easy to relate to the teenagers he mentors, Galindo said.

Gang members first approached Galindo when he was 12, near Newhall Park, while he was walking home from school.

Galindo said he was thankful to have a strict father, a migrant farmer, who kept him from joining.

"I feared my father more than I feared the gang," Galindo said, laughing. It was common to see gang members selling drugs near his home. Some nights, he would sleep on the floor: If gunshots rang out, it was safer to be close to the ground. "It's hard growing up living in fear of getting shot, and living in fear of gangs," Galindo said. "It's easy to get caught up in the gang lifestyle. Knowing how much I struggled, I realize how important it is to have positive role models."

Galindo got involved in sports in high school, and his father's strong influence kept him out of trouble. But the gang life was always just steps away. After high school, Galindo took classes at California State University, Northridge, eventually earning a master's degree. He also worked two jobs, tutoring and doing landscape maintenance. The three survived on very little. For all the problems the neighborhood continues to endure, the hard-working community members take care of each other. Neighbors would bring the three teenagers groceries, he said.

"The community is engulfed in that culture of giving," Galindo, now 32, said this week. "We didn't have much of anything but somehow we managed through it." Galindo still lives in his parents' home about a block from the community center. The negative perception of East Newhall is changing, Galindo said. And officers say crime in the area has decreased. The completion of the new, larger community center on Railroad Avenue has provided kids who would otherwise get in trouble on the street or caught up with gangs a place to come play sports, officials said.

For months, Galindo and Santa Clarita community preservation officers have been walking door-to-door, meeting residents to tell them about programs the city and Santa Clarita Valley Sheriff's Station offer to help improve the neighborhood. Building trust between residents, the city and law enforcement is crucial to improving safety, said Deputy Joe Trejo, who was assigned to the local Sheriff's Station in 1994.

"A lot of these folks are not just from Mexico, they're from different parts of South America where you can't trust the government, and you can't trust police," Trejo said. "We want to let them know that's not how it is here." More work ahead. Despite improvements, gangs are still a powerful influence in the area. Children are recruited at a young age to sell drugs, Trejo said. "There's more peer pressure (from gangs) nowadays," Trejo said. "Gang members have learned that the drug trade is profitable. They don't care if a kid gets in trouble for selling drugs for them."

Someone like Galindo, who chose to stay in school

instead of joining a gang, has a profound impact on children being pressured to join up, Trejo said. "Efren grew up out here and shows these kids that they can aspire to work for the city or become a deputy," Trejo said. "In areas like East Newhall that are underprivileged, you want to show them that you can make it big out there." That's what Galindo is hoping for.

"If I tell my story, (maybe) people can get something out of it," Galindo said. "Sometimes you have to live through it to understand it."

******

Hopelessness

The most devastating effect of a destroyed value system comes when a person decides that there is no longer any hope of ever securing a value system that can supply their need. Once confidence in the traditional value system is lost, social and relationship boundaries quickly begin to fall. That is usually followed by an attitude of "I don't care anymore about anyone or anything other than getting what pleases me, today". It reminds me of the chorus for a country song that I heard recently; it goes a little like this: "when everything is gone, anything goes".

Some years ago I stumbled upon a televised report from the head of a community social reform program. The program chairman was reporting on the success of a community's social services programs. He was giving his opinion as to why the programs seemed to be making little or no difference in the community. His comment was startling and profound. He said that he finally realized that the people had simply lost hope. They had given up on the prospect of life ever getting any better, and consequently, they just lived for the day. They simply expected no future for themselves beyond tomorrow and therefore had no use for any program that extended beyond that day. That foundation of hopelessness ruled their value system and they had fully accepted it. Their value systems were adapted to their day-to-day circumstances.

******

In one of my mentoring encounters with Kendall, I was confronted with just that. The young man simply came out and said, "I just don't care anymore". My response to him was, "hold on a minute, we need to stop the train and back up". I told him that if he no longer cared, we were both wasting our time. I knew that unless I could get him to care again, my time and efforts would be completely futile. Fortunately, after a few minutes of encouraging words and letting him know that I would always be there for support, I was able to restore his hope. At this point, (nearly three years later), he is nearing the end of his prison term and still has a positive outlook for his future.

******

When a young person decides that they must adjust their value system, the new system is created from *their* assessment of their experiences, resources, and personality. The foundation of that new value system will be based on their *perception* of their experiences, their immaturity, and education. It will also reflect the unique aspects of their gender. Once a new values system takes over, it is not likely to have all of the society-friendly boundaries and ethics that are deemed acceptable by mainstream society. After all, society's value system has failed them. The core of this new system is almost completely self-centered.

Usually that new value system will include methods that will quickly restore some sense of security and physical needs. That system can be criminal, or be an open door to it. Since retaliation is natural to us, a tendency to turn to crime is not all that surprising, particularly for young men. To begin with, inexperience and immaturity provides a false sense of confidence, believing they are smart enough not to get caught-or in some cases, not to get caught again.

Chapter 5

Mortal Morality

"During times of universal deceit, telling the truth becomes a revolutionary act".

George Orwell

On my way home one day I spotted church sign that read, "If the truth hurts, it should". We live in an America now where everybody jumps up and down because someone gets offended or claim they have been discriminated against when someone says something they don't like. It seems that too many times the things that offend people are things pertaining to godly morality or spiritual truths.

Noted author and speaker Dr. Miles Monroe said, "Whatever becomes accepted as a norm in our society eventually becomes the law of the land". The spirit of that truth is very evident in our moral laws. Our communities, as well as our nation, are good pictures of that in terms of whatever morality code we have left. The basis of the problem is quite simple. As I mentioned earlier, now that we've managed to wipe out any reference to God and His morality, we are replacing it with our own. Unless it comes from a source higher than all of us it is flawed.

Furthermore, if any code of morality lacks commitment and sacrifice, it is of little value.

Part of the reason we are facing this juvenile crisis is a result of what happens when God and the bible are made to be irrelevant. Many have developed their morality based on personal experiences and human wisdom. Human pride makes us believe that we are smart enough that we don't need any direction from a source higher than us. Consequently, our morality gets adjusted down to the limits of our own wisdom and vision. From where I'm standing, that seems to be coming up a little short. It seems that nearly every time we find ourselves in a bad situation that requires commitment, discipline, pain, and/or hardship, we adjust our value system. Taking the easy way out has become the norm.

Just a few decades ago, pre-marital sex, unwed mothers, disrespect for elders, and casual divorces were considered shameful things. Now they are as acceptable as going to the grocery store. As our value system has eroded, these and many others like them have become commonplace and acceptable. Our new value system looks for ways to get the benefits of a godly value system from an ungodly one. The quick and easy way out is mirrored in our country's approach to dealing with our physical health.

There is overwhelming evidence that most of our physical problems are a result of denying several basic health rules. Poor habits in regard to sleep, diet, water intake, and exercise are good places to start. Rather than change these habits and move back to a healthy lifestyle, most of us will go to our early grave taking tons of pills and various medications instead. These only temporarily mask the pain and symptoms, while causing more harm to our bodies than the sickness itself. Likewise, as we abandon the old value systems for the new, easier ones, we put our families and communities on a fast track to destruction. Since social programs treat the symptoms, our communities' problems linger and grow.

I take advantage of every opportunity I have to express to young teens my philosophy as to why they should keep from premarital sex. Crude grammar aside, it goes something like this: "Sex is for married folks and marriage is for grown folks-and you ain't neither one".

We learn at an early age that our decisions carry consequences. Corporal punishment and the revoking of privileges are usually our first experiences as such. So, once again I revisit the question, "why does this child continue to do wrong, knowing the consequences; I know he knows better?" The answer: a new value system.

Chapter 6

Painful Decisions

"Where there is anger, there is always pain underneath."

-Eckhart Tolle

The decisions we make are the main things that determine the ups and downs, ins and outs, joys and fears, and successes and failures of our lives. With the importance of decision making so obvious why do we make so many bad ones? Nearly all of the decisions we make that have any real effect on our lives are based on two things, 1) information, and 2) emotions. Almost without fail, if we get good information, along with balanced emotions, we will make good decisions. However, when good information is present, the majority of our problems come by way of decisions made from an unbalanced emotional state. These comfortable, short term decisions are destructive in the long run.

In teens, and some adults, far too many decisions are based on emotions. Most of the important decisions in life must be made completely apart from all emotions. When our value system breaks down, our emotions are ignited beyond what is normal. Then our coping mechanisms go to work to try and bring them under control. Satisfying those emotions becomes our first priority.

When a child endures a high level of trauma, it typically results in distress that leads to emotional imbalance. Emotional damage that goes unchecked (unhealed) will pave the way for a new, distorted value system, resulting in choices that often defy reason. For instance, many women who have been abused continue to get into abusive relationships. Some have even testified that abuse is the only thing they are comfortable with. Their distorted value system makes them feel that abuse is a show of love. Even those who aren't comfortable with it often have a difficult time changing the behavior that attracts it. When the value system breaks down and the feeling of security is gone, fear begins to take over. Before very long, the victim will find a way to take control, and that control is now king. In a kingdom mentality, whatever the king says do, you do it.

Far too often the end game is criminal activity. In the confusion of pain and frustration, one thing remains clear. They feel hurt and betrayed, and their subsequent criminal actions are an attempt to deal with that pain and/or vent frustration.

In this new value system a demand for fairness and retaliation moves to the front of the class. As a child, when someone hit us, our natural reaction was to hit back. It is a concept of fairness that is natural to all of us. When a person endures a level of unfairness the natural reaction is retaliation, or in some way recover what they feel was taken from them. The subconscious mind says,"Someone owes me something".

If fairness cannot be achieved in connection with the offender, then the next available person or opportunity will do just fine. That feeling often goes hand-in-hand with symptoms of laziness and irresponsibility. The offended person's distorted value system leads them to decide that since they can't get what they deserve from the offender, the next target is society in general.

Most drug companies thrive on our quick-fix, easy way out mentality. There is a drug or pill available for virtually every major or minor pain we find ourselves faced with. If that's not enough, it seems that some drug companies will be happy to make up an ailment or two if you need one. Many of these symptoms find their way into the "disease" column. Often, the drug's side-effects, many rather severe, takes longer to list that what the drug is supposed to treat. Yet, the drugs are being sucked down in record numbers. The goal is to quickly ease physical pain, and worry about the side effects later.

This same thing goes on in our world of emotions. These emotional pains must be dealt with quickly and easily in order for us to remain sane and re-establish a feeling of security.   To cope, we mask our pain with pleasures of alcohol, drugs, sexual gratification, money, fame, possessions, power, and criminal behavior. These temporary remedies ultimately cause deeper pain later on, often taking one back to the "medications" just mentioned, but in a much higher dosage.

Might I remind you, sexual activity has been the most popular short-term pain killer since the beginning of mankind. It is the number one prescribed medicine by our "internal" pharmacist. But like most pain killers, the side effects of its improper use are evident in the ills of our society. That laundry list of ills includes, but is not limited to:

Child Abandonments
Children out of wedlock
Children raising children
Women degradation
Child exploitation
Marital infidelity
Teenage pregnancies

STD's
Sterility from STD's
Too many grandmothers raising grandsons
******

The young man I talked about earlier, Kendall, at one point had that quick-fix mindset. He said that when he got out of prison his plan was to quickly get the cash needed in order to get set up. Getting a job would take too long. His plan was to resume his drug dealing. However, this time he would be smarter. He told me that the main reason most drug dealers get caught is that they get greedy, and don't know when to pull out. His plan was to make a certain amount of cash, then pull out before he gets caught again.

******

There is another factor that is a part of a new value system that is also extremely important- control.

The element of extreme control is not necessary in a proper functioning value system. After experiencing hurt or trauma, we understand that there are two elements to blame:

1) Someone else caused our trauma.

2) We were unable to stop it.

Once we are older and have more ability and resources, we exercise whatever control we can find. The goal is to ensure that we never again endure that kind of pain. The move is from helplessness to power, physically and emotionally.

This control can take on various forms. Included can be accumulation of money, gang affiliation, abuse of others, running away, criminal activity, and prostitution-all the way up to suicide. I found it astonishing that one traumatized young lady who abused herself by cutting her own flesh with sharp objects had an interesting perspective to her new value system. As physically painful as the cutting was, she felt a sense of security in the idea that at least this was a pain she could control.

Many years ago, I heard a mind-bending story of a woman's battle with a physical ailment that kept her in constant, intense pain. The doctors had done all they could do. As the woman was literally losing her mind, the doctors finally said that there was only one thing left to do. However, it came with potentially dangerous consequences. Since all pain is transmitted through the nervous system, the only thing left to do was to disconnect the nervous system. It is called a cordotomy.

Cordotomy: the surgical cutting of certain nerve fibers of the spinal cord to ease untreatable pain.

This procedure would definitely stop the pain. In fact, it would stop all pain and virtually all physical sensations. As much as pain may be undesirable, it is necessary for our survival. It is the body's way of signaling that something is wrong. After a cordotomy, that natural warning system is no longer working. You could be leaning on a hot stove or stepping on a nail piercing your foot, and you wouldn't feel it. You could die from a clot in your brain because you would feel no headache to alert you to get medical attention.

This woman was in such pain that she chose the cordotomy. Many people resort to "emotional" cordotomies. The emotional pain sometimes becomes unbearable and for some the coping mechanism is simple, turn it all off. Ignoring the pain is a way of pretending that it never happened and is another way of gaining control. As a result, a person's decisions and actions often seem to go against reason and common sense.

When it comes to making many important decisions, what we believe or how we perceive situations may be the most important element of all. People make decisions based largely on what they *perceive* to be reality. Reality can vary from person to person because it is a product of age, personality, maturity, education, experience and facts. The added affects of trauma and abuse further distorts perception. Distorted perception is a false reality, and can lead to deception.

A person who has undergone a physical cordotomy now has a false perception of physical reality. If you ask them how they feel, they will say, "fine". The damage of the pain that is being masked is still going on. The emotional cordotomy has the same effect. When a person is deceived about reality, bad decisions are often the result. The lines get blurred between truth and falsehood, needs and wants, love and lust. At its extreme, right and wrong get reversed.

Chapter 7

For Ladies Only

I had a young man tell me one time that he never wants to have pre-marital sex with a virgin. When I asked why he said, "If you do, they cling to you and you can't get rid of them".

I had to ask myself why that might be. Could it be that the bible is right when it teaches that the sexual experience was designed to be a lifelong covenant relationship between husband and wife? Could ignoring that be the reason most women feel so betrayed? For some that conclusion may not go over very well- the real, hard truths rarely do. The worst part is I'm not sure who is more upset at that statement-the boys or the girls! As a result, some will sacrifice the most precious thing they have for a short-lived, life-changing experience that they *thought* was love.

One of the most precious things that women have is their sexuality. It is at the very core of their self-esteem. It is an integral part of their emotional and psychological well-being. As we have devalued it with casual and pre-marital sex, many women have come to regard that as "that's just the way life is". We have our music and other media industries as main supporters of this ideology-after all, sex sells. Society has disregarded the God-ordained covenant of sex from its rightful place of marriage. It is now accepted as a casual, recreational sport for the young and old. It has resulted in many shattered lives of young girls and families.

Responsibility and sacrifice are no longer options for our new mentality. We have reduced godliness to whatever philosophy that suits our fancy. *Abstinence doesn't suit our fancy.* As a result, the "weight" of our sexual attitudes always falls back onto the female.

She has her virginity stolen-more so by society's lie, than by the boy's lie. She is the one who has to deal with the sorrow of losing her self-esteem. (All too often her self-esteem was already gone). She is the one who has to physically endure the pregnancy as well as the birth pains. She is the one who has to manage the sleepless nights of breastfeeding. She is the one pushing the stroller down the street, on the bus, to the store. She is the one who often becomes that target of her son's anger if she even mentions the dad's irresponsibility. She is the one who has to try to comfort her son about his dad's absence. She is the one who sometimes begins to neglect her son as she reaches out to another man to capture a taste of life's pleasures while "she's still got it". And when it has come full circle, she is the one crying, watching her son being carried off to jail.

-Remix: when the boy gets out of jail, he finds the next desperate, love-starved girl looking to reconstruct her value system: repeat the cycle.-

After much disappointment, abuse and failed relationships, many women have lost any hope of ever having a sound relationship with men. However, they still desire to be a mother. Some act on the notion that the only thing they need from a man is his sperm. They often purposely launch into single parenthood, confident they can raise a child all on their own. Some launch into it simply because they expect that child to be a source of unconditional love that was never gotten from their father. For some it provides a sense of self-worth and significance.

Simply said, single parenting is not something one should plan to do! When women do that on purpose, often the early years of raising that son are full of love and purpose. Without sufficient male nurturing, that son will have an extremely high probability of being the source of much heartache and tears in the years to come.

There is yet another dark side of this psychological fallout that many women get exposed to when raising a son alone. I've seen and heard of numerous instances of mothers being mistreated by the very son they raised, loved, and protected. There are countless cases where the parents are separated for justifiable reasons. Needless to say, the mother is stunned and confused when the son turns on her, often blaming her for the separation, not really caring who caused it.

Often that hurt and anger gets vented toward the person that has truly loved and cared for them the most, their mother. Remember I talked earlier about feeling hurt and wanting to hurt someone back. Combine that with the fact that mothers typically are the ones who are "softer" on the children. Now mix in the reality that boys usually don't respond to the discipline from the mother the same way they do from the father. Then consider that fact that the natural nurturing from the mother can come across as a weakness. Therefore, many times that mother, who seems the weakest, becomes the target. Understand, in the eyes of the son, if dad isn't at fault, mom is the next suspect. Again, often the son doesn't care to know who's at fault; he simply acts out his feelings on the next closest person.

The father-son bond can be so strong in some boys that regardless of the facts, they simply cannot, or will not, see the fault in the father. Sometimes even when they see it, their strong desire for their father's love and acceptance still overrides any fault the father may have.

Some sons endure rejection from their fathers for years before they accept that their father will never be a father to them. Some never get over it. When they carry that anger and hurt into their own future families the dysfunction often gets repeated! That is just another astounding mystery of the human psyche. In frustration, we tend to repeat bad behaviors that we have experienced if they are not resolved.

Some don't get the opportunity to pass it on to their families. That pain and frustration gets acted out in juvenile activity. That often results in an extended life of crime and jail time, preventing them from ever having a family.

And every step of the way, these sons truly love their mothers dearly. It is a prime example of how the human psyche seems to operate in a way that seems to contradict itself. It is a picture of irrational thinking, reasoning, and acting- a product of a distorted value system.

******

The following is an excerpt from an article written by a former worker in the Montessori pre-school academy about the important role of fathers.

My Father, *this* side of Heaven

My work with children has poignantly shown me
the importance of having dads in our children's lives.
Divorces break the marital bond, but don't allow them to
break the parenting bond. Healthy, engaged dads give our
children 5 important gifts. These gifts are:

1. A sense of protection. Dads are bigger and physically
stronger than moms. Kids who don't have a dad in the
home frequently tell me they feel unsafe.

2. Dad is usually more playful with the kids. Play is a child's
work. It is very important for healthy growth and
development. It is also a wonderful way for children to
bond with their dad.

3. Healthy dads model respect for women by how they
treat the child's mother. No one has more influence on
how to treat women in our society and families than dads.
When you see a child who doesn't respect their mother or
other women, watch their dad.

4. An engaged, loving dad is a strong predictor for girls to
delay having sex, and also making wiser choices with
relationships.

5. An engaged, healthy dad is the best role model for
raising a son who will practice the morals and values
passed on to him. Dads also teach daughters how all men
should behave toward her. If a dad is attentive and

engaged with his daughter, he is the one who sets the bar high for whom his daughter will date in the future.

Matthew and his dad did talk, not once, but frequently. Dad learned he didn't need to leave his son just because he left his mother. Mom continues to grow and struggle with her fear of losing Matthew. Mom understands that in order to be healthy, Matthew needs both his mom and dad. I asked her the most painful part of the experience she has been through. She told me, "I have to focus on loving Matthew more than I focus on resenting his father for what he did to me." I told her that by doing this one action, she was showing Matthew what a parent's love really is.

******

Crossroads, a United Way mentoring program has as its motto: "Mentor one child, change two lives". Conversely, most women who don't understand the important relationship between a boy and his father will likely have their motto as: "I raised my son thinking he didn't really need a father, and now I've ruined *two* lives".

Recently, I had what I thought were some interesting questions come to mind, i.e., "Why is it that the mothers always get the major burden in raising the child alone? Why can't the father be the primary caretaker? Why is it that the (young) mother's life is put on hold while the father gets to continue to party, come home when or if he wants to, and generally gets to "do his thing"? What would be wrong with, (after the baby is weaned), giving him to the father to be raised"?

Looking from a different angle, here are perhaps some advantages. In most cases, the men will get higher paying jobs, with the ability to provide a better economic situation. When the child has to be carried, the men are typically stronger and better suited for such. Men usually can provide more adequate physical protection for the child. Oh yes, the x-factor, nurturing. Are women really better suited? Good question. It's probably safe to say that in the infant and early childhood stages women are more capable. However, as that son approaches the teen years the connection with his father becomes more and more crucial each day. It is a transition period in life where the attributes of being a man are beginning to take shape. Having a man in his life to model himself after is critical.

******

A former neighbor of mine was talking about her adolescent sons, whom she raised without their father. She recounted how during the early years of the boy's lives, things were going well and she was quite proud of how she had managed to keep them headed in the right direction. Needless to say, she dropped her voice and lamented how the tide changed when they reached their teen years. What had seemed to be such a success story was rapidly changing into despair, as one son began wandering around with no direction, and the other began to flirt with the criminal justice system. She wonders out loud about what she did wrong. Truth is, it probably had nothing to do with what she did, but rather more of what she couldn't do-be a father.

******

Now I understand how difficult it would be for most mothers to give up custody of their child. I'm not suggesting that it is always best or necessary. What I am saying is that it is of extreme importance for that son to spend more time with his father than just every other month, or every other weekend for that matter.

Whether or not that involves a new custody agreement is not the point. Simply find a way to increase dad's involvement in the son's life-whatever it takes. In today's society, even with good, strong fathers *in* the home, it is still sometimes barely enough to keep that son from running with the wrong crowd and finding his way into the juvenile system.

It is common to watch the single mom work very hard, long hours, sometimes even two jobs, trying to provide the basic needs for her sons. She showers them with love, and dedicates whatever spare time she can find to support them. But with her salary, money will only go for the basics, trying desperately to save for Christmas or a rainy day. Then when the oldest wants to play little league sports, mom says no. It's too expensive and there's just no room for such activities. Besides, there is the problem of transportation and injuries, and perhaps there is no insurance coverage. Lastly, he needs to be there to take care of the younger siblings.

There are many adult athletes who will testify that their participation in sports gave them an opportunity to release that tension, anger and hurt surrounding their absentee father. Many have admitted that involvement in sports played a large part in keeping them from criminal activities.

A former co-worker told me about his parent's philosophy. Since both were teachers, education was a priority for them. However, they also believed that those extra activities were nearly as important to their children's welfare and overall development as academics. Both areas help to create well-rounded children. Consequently, when discipline was necessary, taking away participation in sports or other similar activities was usually a last resort.

******

I recount a story I recently read concerning a young man having a successful college football career here in Houston. He and his two older brothers were being raised by their mom. While still in grade school, the youngest son pleaded with his mom to play football. The busy working mother's answer was a resounding, "NO, I don't have the time, money, or energy- and besides, you are too little and you might get hurt". Well, the two older brothers had a different idea. They reasoned, "What mom doesn't know won't hurt her". They secretly signed up little brother in Pop-Warner football and took him to games and practices. They used a friend's house as a "locker room", and created various excuses for the bumps and bruises that came from football. Believe it or not, they were successful at this covert operation nearly all the way through high school. As fate would have it, near the end of his high school playing career, his football success eventually wound up in the newspaper and the cat was out of the bag.

It didn't take long for mom to accept the reality and begin to fully support her youngest son. The question is, had the big brothers not stepped in and allowed little brother that opportunity, what turn might the boy have taken?

******

One of my own sons, who will testify that I was a pretty good father (I think), told me that had it not been for sports, he likely would have been a statistic also. I know that sports are not a cure-all, and it is certainly not for every child. Nevertheless, not only children, but adults as well, need something in our lives to look forward to. Activities not only help to relieve tension, but also provide a healthy way for self expression. It simply is a part of a well-balanced mentality. Let me remind you of the saying that most of us are familiar with; an idle mind is the devil's workshop.

Often, mothers don't realize that the adrenaline and testosterone building inside that son needs an outlet. They don't understand that participation in extra-curricular activities can be a great outlet to balance the physical and emotional welfare of those sons. To her it's just something fun to do, but unnecessary.

Beware: that adrenaline and testosterone will come to the surface. Many times it will surface in the form of unhealthy or criminal behavior. I have come across several mothers whose oldest son is now in jail, and she is right back where she started. Again there is a need for someone to help raise the two younger siblings. Now there is the extra burden of trying to hang on to the older one.

Having a good male figure in a son's life needs to be top priority! Remember the saying, "pay me now or pay me later?" Usually, the later cost is much, much higher.

Chapter 8
For Men Only

Just as it is important for the father to be in the home, it is equally important how he manages the home. We are divinely warned as fathers "not to exasperate (create undue stress and trauma) your children".

The words that are said, or not said, factor greatly in the character and development of a child. On several occasions I have asked fathers how often they praise their sons. Often the answer is, "when he does something worthy of my praise, then he'll get it".

Let me suggest a better approach. Praise your son just for who he is. Find anything, no matter how small, and praise him over it. Take the opportunity when nothing good or bad has happened to tell your son how proud you are of him.

Praise will cause him to try to live up to the attitude you have of him. Diligently look for times to praise your son. He will love it and he needs it and will respond to it. Make up a situation if necessary. Highlight the strengths and downplay the weaknesses.

******

My Father, *this* side of Heaven

There was an incident in Houston a few years back where two teenagers managed to rescue a teacher from an attempted assault. While being praised on the news as heroes, the interviewer asked what their parents thought of their efforts. One of the sixteen-year olds responded by saying, "it is the first time my father has ever said that he is proud of me".

******

It has been estimated that roughly ninety to ninety-five percent of men serving time have testified that while they were growing up, they were constantly told, "one day you will end up in jail". The things that are said to you by someone you respect and look up to can play a large role in the direction of your life. Too many times the mother will notice that her son's actions are beginning to resemble the destructive past of the absent father. Although said with the good intention of discouraging the bad behavior, often the wrong thing is said such as,"You're going to be just like your father". It is more profitable not to speak of and reinforce past behavior, but rather speak of the desired good behavior.

Most of us know of personal experiences where fathers have compared one son that he is proud of to another son he is not so proud of by saying things like, "You'll never measure up to your brother"; or "Why can't you be more like him"?   A few simple words can tip the scale of a child's life to an attitude of success, or help pave a path to failure.

******

Some time ago a bible study teacher of mine shared with the class a personal story of the power of words. He recounted that he grew up with a father who was always there and was a good provider. Unfortunately his father rarely, if ever communicated with his children on a personal level. While obviously still dealing with his own childhood trauma of spending time in an orphanage, his father was a strict disciplinarian. He sometimes threatened the children with being shipped to an orphanage for severe misbehavior.

As a youngster, Bill was a leading participant in his local Boy Scout troop and was primed to be one of the select few to go on a special hiking trip, which only some could qualify for. At the last minute, Bill's father told him that he couldn't go. Upon asking why, the father replied, "you're not good enough". Crushed and confused, Bill spent most of his adult life overcoming the weight of those words.

******

I know personally of a situation where even though the father had a choice, he preferred the night work schedule as opposed to the day schedule. The father simply liked it better. It resulted in him having very little opportunity to spend quality time with his son who was being raised almost exclusively by the mother. As the son reached his teenage years, dad noticed that his son had more of his mother's traits than his. When you have a choice, opt for whatever allows more time with your son. If you don't have a choice, make sure that you maximize the time with your son that you do have.

******

In the midst of all of this I find that there are still a number of men who have a sincere desire to be a father to their sons but somehow miss the simplest ingredient: spending quality time *with* their sons. Stories continue to pop up about the father who works long, long hours to provide upper-class housing and a lot of material things for their sons, and yet are confused when the son goes out and robs and steals. Unfortunately in our society, many professions do not allow time enough for family. Either the amount of hours at work or the schedule gets in the way. Sometimes that is simply unavoidable.

Tragically, many fathers did not find out until it was too late that their sons needed their *presence* much, much more than they needed their *presents*. One of the great classic songs concerning this subject is called "Cats in the Cradle", by Harry Chapin. It would be well worth your

My Father, *this* side of Heaven

time to find it and listen to it.   Until then, here are the
lyrics.

My child arrived just the other day
He came to the world in the usual way
But there were planes to catch and bills to pay
He learned to walk while I was away
And he was talkin' 'fore I knew it, and as he grew
He'd say "I'm gonna be like you dad
You know I'm gonna be like you"

And the cat's in the cradle and the silver spoon
Little boy blue and the man on the moon
When you comin' home dad?
I don't know when, but we'll get together then son
You know we'll have a good time then

My son turned ten just the other day
He said, "Thanks for the ball, Dad, come on let's play
Can you teach me to throw", I said "Not today
I got a lot to do", he said, "That's ok"
And he walked away but his smile never dimmed
And said, "I'm gonna be like him, yeah
You know I'm gonna be like him"

Well, he came home from college just the other day
So much like a man I just had to say
"Son, I'm proud of you, can you sit for a while?"
He shook his head and said with a smile

My Father, *this* side of Heaven

"What I'd really like, Dad, is to borrow the car keys
See you later, can I have them please?"

And the cat's in the cradle and the silver spoon
Little boy blue and the man on the moon
When you comin' home son?
I don't know when, but we'll get together then son
You know we'll have a good time then
I've long since retired, my son's moved away
I called him up just the other day
I said, "I'd like to see you if you don't mind"
He said, "I'd love to, Dad, if I can find the time
You see my new job's a hassle and kids have the flu
But it's sure nice talking to you, Dad
It's been sure nice talking to you"

And as I hung up the phone it occurred to me
He'd grown up just like me
My boy was just like me

******

One of the most unfortunate things about our psychological makeup is how easily we are deceived by materials things. Sometimes the food, clothing, or shelter comes up a little short of what we desire, and even sometimes what we need. Our misperception is that lack of money and stuff is the reason for our unhappiness. That wrong emotional perception drives us to overly cherish and rely on material things to fill feelings of emptiness. A solid family relationship can prevent that from being an emotional pitfall.

******

A powerful story was related to me that was one of the saddest I had ever heard. A young man recalled that while growing up, his father was an excellent provider but it came at the cost of countless hours at work, leaving almost no time for family interaction. His father's personality was highlighted by his habit to keep an hourly notebook of **every** day's activities. By some unknown prompting, the father decided to take off from his always busy schedule and take his 10 year-old son fishing. To the son, being able to spend half a day with his dad was something he thought would never happen. It was an event he treasured with all of his heart. Somewhat like the father, the son noted in his memory every detail of that day and locked it away as the biggest treasure of his childhood.

Many years later, the father passed away. While thinking of his childhood, the son remembered that his father noted the events of every day in his past. He decided to search his fathers' daily record book and relive that cherished fishing trip. He could hardly wait to see the joy that his father expressed in his book about that day.

He found the book and searched back to that day. His father's entry read, "Spent nearly all day fishing- a totally wasted day."

******

An article in the Houston Chronicle newspaper put it this way:

For you, I offer these 10 commandments of righteous fatherhood. Pay close attention, because, behind your back, people are pitying your wife:

1. No golf on weekends: Seriously, it's ludicrous. Your spouse is home with the kids all the time, and you think it's OK to take five hours on a weekend day to pursue your own pastime? Selfishness, thy name is Father.

2. Wake up: Literally, wake up. With your kids. On at least one of the two weekend days -- and perhaps both. I know: you wake up early for work. Not even remotely the same thing. Rising alongside the kiddies is hard. And crazy. And (gasp!) sorta fun, if you'd just stop moping.

3. Change diapers: If you have little kids, and you don't know how to change diapers (or, even worse, refuse to change diapers), you're pathetic. That's no exaggeration -- p-a-t-h-e-t-i-c. It's not all that hard, and though the poop

sometimes winds up on the fingers, well, uh, yeah. It just does. Wash your hands.

4. Play with dolls and paint your toenails: How many fathers do I know who refuse to get girlish with their girls? Dozens. Dude, put aside the machismo, break out Barbie and slather on some pink polish. You'll make a friend for life -- and nobody else is watching.

5. Do things you don't want to do: It's easy to take the kids to the driving range -- because you want to be there. Now try spending the day having a tea party at American Girl. Or crawling through one of those wormholes at the nearby kiddie gym. Fun? Often, no. But this isn't about you.

6. Order the wife to bug off: I recently met a mother who told me her husband hadn't been alone with their 9-year-old daughter for more than two hours ... ever. Inexcusable. Let your wife do her own thing: relax, take a run, whatever. Entertain your children solo. They don't bite (Note: CNN.com is not liable if your children do, in fact, bite).

7. Surprise! Just once, on a random day without meaning or purpose, show up early at your kid's school/camp/wherever, say "Get in the car!" and take

him/her somewhere special. Just the two of you, alone. A movie. A park. A hike. The memory lasts -- I promise.

8. Dishes Don't Clean Themselves (Nor Do Toys): It's amazing how this one works. You pick up a dish, run it under hot water with some soap, rub it down with a towel and place it back on the shelf. Then repeat.

9. Wake up your kid: Not often. But if you want to score big points and create a killer memory moment, walk in Junior's room at, oh, midnight, wake him/her up and go outside for 10 minutes to watch the stars.

10. For God's sake, tell your kids you love them: They never see you, and they'd probably like to know.

Bud, as you read this your wife is expecting little -- and your kids are expecting even less. Pull one out of the blue. Make Father's Day less about you, and all about them.

******

On that note, there is one other area where the men must step up. I often hear men bragging about how they have fulfilled their responsibility by paying their child support. While that is certainly admirable, that is only half of the story. I believe there are a ton of fatherless boys out there who would tell you that if they could choose, they'd rather have your presence than your money.   (Of course, the financially strapped mother may not agree).

A good friend of mine told me of a trip he took to Miami, Florida a few years back.   While attending an exclusive night club, he had an opportunity to meet and talk with some of the most beautiful women he had ever seen. This club was a common hangout for professional athletes. Many of these women confessed to him that their goal was to find an athlete, any athlete, to father their child. Their only goal was to secure a wealthy lifestyle from the child support. As we all know, many athletes have fallen victim to those few moments of pleasure. In my opinion, this qualifies as legal exploitation of children. They are basically being brought into the world explicitly for financial gain, resulting from selfish women who seduce weak-minded men.

The most precious things in life can't be bought with money, and there may be nothing more precious than the relationship between a father and son.

Chapter 9

Village People

Back to the artificial biscuits-they are better than nothing. Enter the mentors. Though mentors are far from artificial, they can provide a father-like covering for young men who are without a father. Imperfect and incomplete families will always be a part of life, this side of heaven. Nevertheless, the old African proverb, "It takes a village to raise a child", expresses how our communities need to be on board to assist families. For societies to function properly, they need communities to be on board.

******

Making Mighty Men

(Augusta, Ga., 2001)

Rick Keuroglian, middle-age and balding, holds a laptop in his right arm. He begins by talking about a passage from the Bible — one from the book of Acts. The lesson is a simple one; it's about motivation. In a quick give-and-take in which he uses a teen's favorite football team as an example, Keuroglian tells the young men they must go from a place of being ordered to do things by adults to a place of wanting to do them for their own sake.

It's probably not the typical way a teenager would spend a Thursday night, but then again, what Keuroglian is doing isn't exactly typical. An active member of the community and president of the Olde Town Neighborhood Association, Keuroglian, whose day job is director of evangelism and community involvement at First Presbyterian Church on Telfair Street, wants to stop his neighborhood's crime at the source, and save a few lives in the process.

Last summer, he began a mentoring program called Making Mighty Men, in which his inaugural class of four teenage boys learned job skills and leadership development. "It's not all about looking out for bad guys," Keuroglian said. "It's about volunteering. It's what can you do to curb crime."

City leaders often emphasize the important role that good parenting and supervision play in keeping children and teenagers away from crime. Sheriff Ronnie Strength said a cultural shift has led to fewer two-parent families and to a lack of traditional values.

Willie Battle, of Men Making a Difference, spends every Wednesday and Friday in Richmond County Juvenile Court, looking for young men his group can help. They are mentored by volunteers, in the hopes that they won't return to the juvenile justice system.

Through tutoring and strong adult male supervision, Battle said, volunteers hope to instill a sense of purpose and discipline that was lacking. Asked what he wants to do with his life, 14-year old Tyrone enthusiastically said he wants be a lawyer. Tyrone, who has been in Keuroglian's program since summer, said he used to get in fights for "no reason." Now the teen responds to questions with a polite "Yes, sir" and says he has found God. " When I was hanging in my other neighborhood, I never heard anyone want to teach me about God. They just wanted to teach me about being a thug and a drug dealer," said Tyrone. Rickell Lynn, 15, was frequently suspended from school before he began working with Making Mighty Men, Keuroglian said. Again, fighting was an issue. Now, Rickell said, he just walks away from trouble.

Whether the teens will stay out of trouble is anyone's guess, but Keuroglian said giving them a strong moral and ethical foundation is at the core of what needs to happen.

"This is my dream," he said. "I want to see a whole new group of guys raised up as leaders in this community."

******

It is common for parents to believe they should be all and everything to their children. They want to be the lone ones to instill values, build character, and be the child's source for all they need. Also, with increasing crime rates parents feel the need to keep their children closer than ever. While no one can dispute that reality, it is also unhealthy to raise a child in the social vacuum of mom and dad. On the other hand, in this day of media everywhere, there is hardly any such thing as a social vacuum.

It was a sobering time for me when I came to realize that my sons needed influences other than mine. They sometimes were more receptive of advice in certain areas of their lives from someone other than me. It was then I realized that the natural social system is designed that way. It takes input from extended family members, neighbors, friends, and to a small extent, society in general, to balance out what children need.

I'd like to revisit the statement made by former NBA great Charles Barkley, stating that he was not a role model. While society generalizes the term to mean "good" role model, in reality we all qualify as role models. A role model is nothing more than an example, and EVERYONE is an example of something! If your lifestyles and actions are visible to anyone at all, you are a role model. A role model is not something that you have to actively do; it is simply who and what you are. If people are exposed to you, something will be gleaned from you, good or bad- whether or not you know it or like it. You have no choice about whether or not you are a role model. The only choice you have is what kind of role model you will be-a good one or a bad one.

******

(An excerpt from an article from the magazine <u>The African Executive:</u> See complete article in appendix)

"...Regardless of either outcome, mentors provide the following services to their students: guidance, protection, parenting, nurturing, coaching, advisory, counseling, emotional and financial support, and consulting. Mentors demonstrate the capacities to listen attentively, to observe human conditions from different perspectives, to impart knowledge, to tell stories of their experiences at the right moments and in relevant ways, to exercise a lot of patience, to correct erring behaviors of their students, to do some hand-holding when necessary, to comfort and reassure their students at times of uncertainty and disillusionment, to recognize when change is necessary and must be made, and to build confidence in their students one day at a time. Without a cue from someone else, mentors transition seamlessly into different roles at the right time as a guide, guardian, nurturer, coach, teacher, consultant, counselor, confidence-builder, substitute parent, supporter, friend, and occasionally an antagonist of bad behavior..."

******

In reality parents do not have the ability to completely control who their children model themselves after in every area of life. No matter what parents do or don't do, children will always be exposed to additional role models, such as coaches or teachers or someone in the media. In our media-blitzed world thousands of outside role models are constantly paraded in front of all of us. Even though the children may not necessarily follow directly in the footsteps of a role model they know is bad, a simple unhealthy idea gleaned from that person can have an effect on how they look at life.

Once again, this speaks to the power of subtle things that influence us. Even when brought up with good values, it is natural and normal to look for society to support what is taught at home. When children see successful and prominent people whose lives don't reflect those things, it can plant a seed of doubt in their minds about what is real and necessary. Children need to see the right things modeled by people outside of the home as well as inside. Even with two good parents, other influences can sometimes override what is taught and modeled at home!

******

When one of my sons was in high school dreaming of becoming a professional athlete, he would often watch stories of the lives of successful athletes. After viewing an episode one day, he came to me with a huge sigh of relief. All of the previous shows had featured athletes who had used inspiration from a traumatic or tragic circumstance to help propel them into stardom. On that day he said to me that he had finally seen a story about a successful athlete that came from a good, "normal", home, with no trauma or tragedy. Up until then, he had almost decided that since his life had no serious trauma and tragedy, he wouldn't have the inspiration it took to be a success! That show, (that I thought was good for him), was actually planting seeds of doubt in his mind, and I was completely unaware of it.

My Father, *this* side of Heaven

****

Virtually every person who has any amount of success in anything was aided in some way by someone who wasn't legally obligated to do it. Therefore, I believe each person has a basic moral responsibility to return the favor to society by at least being a good citizen if nothing else. Remember, since we never know who is watching, you never know how your life will influence others, good or bad. So, if the children with "good" parents need additional role models, how much more does that apply to children with "bad" parents or no parents at all?

We are all aware of the concept of "an ounce of prevention is worth a pound of cure". Embracing that ideology is vital to dealing with juvenile delinquency. Again, a large majority of offenders begin their journey into criminal life around the age of 13. Being proactive in finding a mentor before trouble rears its ugly head is the best strategy. I've heard parents testify that they were caught completely off guard in the change of behavior. Many have testified that seemingly overnight their sons went from being this great kid on a good track to a troubled young man.

Finding that big brother/mentor at an early age can be a huge factor keeping boys from going astray. I also know that that is easier said than done, seeing how there are so few men volunteering. Nevertheless, it is something that must be pursued with a lot of effort. Don't wait until trouble rears its ugly head! If the first mentor doesn't work out, try again, and again.

If the son's lack of direction lands him behind bars, now he does have a mentor-his fellow inmate(s). Not only that, but now the chances of him joining a gang just increased dramatically, and the parent has no way of intervening.

Regarding those success stories coming from single parent homes, I am fully convinced that most of them would tell you of the tremendous effort it took for them to overcome the absence of their father. Most only made it with the intervention of some form of male mentoring. Without the involvement of a good father or the intervention of a mentor, most of these young men will wander through our streets aimlessly, or find their way into the juvenile system.

******

With that being said, here is a case of a young man whose parents never married and his father was living across the country. Although the father was diligent in paying his child support and showed concern for his son, the mother was naturally too attached to the son to send him to live with his father. On several occasions the mother secured a mentor for her son, but the son refused to accept him. He rejected any attempts to be mentored. He only wanted HIS dad! This is just one example of the strong natural bond between father and son. Unfortunately, it also opened the door for the son to grow up without that necessary male influence. It comes as no surprise that he has already taken his introductory course into the state juvenile system.

******

One of the most well-known and successful mentoring programs around the country is the Big Brother/Big Sister Organization. Public/Private Ventures is a national research organization with more than 30 years of experience in studying child development and social service issues. As a result of their independent research, the following is part of a brief report regarding the impact of mentoring." Here is an excerpt taken from the Big Brother/Big Sister website:

"...what mattered to the children were not the activities. It was the fact that they had a caring adult in their lives.

Because they had someone to confide in and to look up to, they were, in turn, doing better in school and at home. And at a time in their lives when even small choices can change the course of their future, the Littles were also avoiding violence and substance abuse.

In addition to the lives of Littles being changed for the better, the impact is contagious.

"When Little Brothers and Little Sisters feel good about themselves," said Mathis, "they can positively impact their friends and families, their schools, and their communities. And as this important study has shown, these young people believe in themselves because a Big Brother or Big Sister believed in them."

It is widely accepted that mentoring is an extremely effective tool in helping to guide young men through life. Solid, meaningful relationships form the very basis for quality of life. We all need someone who will listen to us, and not just talk at us. We all need someone to believe in us, and who is committed to us. We need to feel as though someone understands us and empathizes with our situation. That is vital in order for us to thrive.

And last, but certainly not least, we all need to be encouraged. In a nutshell, that is the foundation of mentoring. Once into the teen years, most of these boys have been lectured and preached to endlessly. While that is a necessary part of parenting, it must be balanced with the right amount of listening.

Detention facilities have counselors and therapists to assist in counseling these young men. As far as I can tell, they do the best job they can.   Helpful insight was provided by Mrs. Michelle O'neill, a family psychologist working with juveniles in Houston, Texas. She noted that much of her effectiveness depends on the willing participation of the person being counseled. This presents a big problem. Unless a person really believes that the counselor really cares, they won't let you inside their world. They often only see just someone doing a job they are paid to do. They feel more like a number than a person.

Additionally, it usually takes several months for trust to be established, and many times the boys have moved on before that happens. Never mind the fact that, as one of my mentees told me, "Some things I won't share with the counselor. If I am open and honest I know they will recommend a treatment or send me to a facility that I don't want". Many of these young men know how to manipulate the system to avoid the treatments they don't want.   And if that's not enough, sometimes even the counselors give in to human nature. Their difficult takes sometimes leads them to frustration. It can cause them to exhibit a non-caring attitude toward the very kids they are supposed to help.

Years ago I attended a workshop for people considering adopting children. The session I remember the most was a lecture by an incredible woman who had been a victim of extensive abuse and abandonment as a child. So much in fact that it led to her spending many years in a mental institution, considered a lost soul.

By way of some miracle this woman was somehow restored. After leaving the institution she recovered her life through education and counseling, and is now an advocate for children. The one conclusion she shared that struck me was this: based on her experience she has determined that about ninety-five percent of people who are in mental institutions are there *only* because they had no one to talk to, and really listen to them! Society's two most well-known institutions are prisons and mental wards. Both are overflowing with people who had no one to really listen to them.

It is virtually impossible to underestimate the importance of people talking about their problems and situations. Regardless of the nature of trauma it is one of the first and most important steps in the recovery process. It is a part of that control element of denial. Unfortunately, talking is often the most difficult thing to get people to do.

Trauma victims know that talking about their trauma also means reliving it. Many times they decide it is too painful to do. Secondly, they feel the shame of it and, and it has the effect of lowering a self-esteem that has already bottomed out. Thirdly, discussion opens the door for lack of empathy and possible embarrassment, which makes the victim feel weak, (unmanly when it comes to males), and vulnerable again. And unless there is a trusting relationship, it will not happen.

The result of not talking can be similar to the effect of drinking poison. It slowly eats a person from the inside out. It usually will show itself in various forms of anti-social behavior such as various types of abuse, strained relationships, and even suicide.

Providing a sense of caring and commitment helps to establish trust. That is the stability that mentors can bring to the table. It can be the first step in helping to reconstruct a proper and healthy value system. The consistent presence of a positive role model can go a long way towards offsetting the negative influences that are flooding our homes and communities. More often than not, mentors play a key role in helping to expand a young man's horizon and expose him to things in society and the world that might otherwise have gone unnoticed.

******

Justin, the young man who lost both of his parents revealed to me his talent as an artist. He also expressed his desire to be an auto mechanic. After encouraging him to pursue his passion, I told him that he did not have to limit himself to that one area.   I mentioned that his talents might also enable him to expand his thought process to include designing wheel rims, or even cars! It was obvious from the spark in his eyes that he had never even considered those possibilities!

******

Quite simply we need more men to step up and step in. The desperate shortage of men mentors is such that organizations have resorted to allowing females to mentor young men. Even though they can't model many of the male things that are needed, they can still provide some necessary care and commitment. Mentoring requires a heart that is concerned about our youth, and a decision to get involved. Hats off to these tremendous women!

Concerning the previously mentioned cordotomy, it is a procedure that is irreversible. Emotional cordotomies can be reversed, and mentors play a vital role in that process.

At the beginning of this book, I mentioned that much of this would also apply to young ladies as well, and I will trust that my readers can discern what applies where.

However, I do have one more paradigm to put on the table concerning the young ladies.

All of these mentoring organizations are also involved in providing female mentors to the girls as well. At appropriate ages it can be very helpful for them to have an older male mentor to serve as a father figure. While being aware of the possible problems with such an idea, I know it can work. As a matter of fact, I recently learned that one of my older brothers had mentored a couple of young ladies and had very positive results.

Just as with the boys, the presence of a father in the life of girls is extremely vital. Understandably, it can be a delicate maneuver, but don't simply discount it if there is a man available that is trustworthy, willing, and capable. Remember, that girl needs things from her father that a mother cannot supply.

******

Kids Off the Block
(Taken from the CNN US website, September, 29, 2011)

On the gritty, gang-filled streets of Chicago's Roseland neighborhood, a grandma has launched a one-woman campaign against drugs and violence by inviting troubled youth into her home where she serves up kindness, compassion and food.

They call her "Ms. Diane," and, in the last year alone, she

has helped more than 300 at-risk teens in one of Chicago's most blighted and gang-infested neighborhoods, according to the website for her nonprofit organization, Kids Off the Block.

In a neighborhood where residents lock themselves inside their homes to escape rampant gang violence, Diane Latiker opens her door, inviting gang members to come inside, CNN, which recently featured her as a CNN Hero, reports.

"They say I'm a nut because I let kids into my home who I didn't even know," Latiker, 54, a mom of eight and grandmother of 13, tells CNN. "But I know (the kids) now. And I'll know the new generation."

Latiker writes on her site that her mother, Evangelist Ruth Jackson, told her to "do something with the youth."

That moment, she says, transformed her and gave her a new mission in life.

In 2003, Latiker was concerned her youngest daughter, Aisha, a high school student, would fall into a gang, since gang members lived next door.

"I started taking (Aisha and her friends) to swimming and movies and whatever," Latiker tells CNN. "My mother saw that, and she said: 'Diane, why don't you do something with the kids? They like you and respect you.' "

That's when she launched the community program Kids Off the Block, with the hope that by providing teens who have been in trouble with support and a place to go, she could bring new hope to a community in crisis.

The program started in her living room, but during the following years "my house started bursting at the seams," she tells CNN.

"It doesn't matter where they come from, what they've done," Latiker tells the network. "We've had six gangs in my living room at one time. ... But that was the safe place. And you know what? They respected that."

The South Side neighborhood where Latiker runs her crusade has been hit hard by the recession, and even more so by gun violence. With just one month left in the school year, 118 youth already have been shot in Chicago public schools, according to Chicago Talks.

"How can a kid get a gun like he can get a pack of gum? It's that crazy," Latiker tells CNN.

Latiker told the kids her house was open 24 hours a day, seven days a week. They could come over for food, help with their homework or just to talk about their hopes, dreams and fears, she tells CNN.

"I invited them into my living room," she tells the network. "They all started saying: 'I want to be a doctor. I want to be a rapper. I want to be a singer.' They didn't want to be out here running up and down the street. They wanted to be involved in something."
Eventually, Latiker quit her job as a cosmetologist to focus on the kids full-time. Through the KOB Youth Community Center, she has set up tutoring sessions with teachers and retired educators and has provided job interview training and opportunities to play football, basketball and soccer. Latiker and volunteers also started taking the kids on field trips to museums, movies, skating rinks, water parks and professional sports games.

Every day, 30 to 50 young people show up at the center for tutoring, counseling or activities such as sports, drama, dance or music.
KOB caters to people age 11 to 24, but 80 percent of those in the program are male, Latiker tells CNN. She emphasizes activities that target males because they are most often perpetrating or confronting the violence of the streets.

Maurice Gilchrist, 15, is one teenager who credits Kids Off the Block with turning his life around, CNN reports.

Gilchrist joined a gang when he was 12, and tells the network life in a gang meant looking behind his back every day.

"We always used to jump on people, rob everything, steal," he tells CNN. "Miss Diane, she changed my life. I love her for that."

Chapter 10

Out of the mouth of Babes...

Earlier I talked about how children come to a point where they naturally know what should be included in a value system. Posted on the wall at the Harris County, Texas juvenile facility are two posters. The incarcerated youths were asked what *they* thought should be proper attributes of a good father and a good mother. Below is what they wrote.

A Good mother

Will whip her child, but don't just beat them for no reason.

Go to the child's open house at school.

Won't leave her child alone for long periods of time.

Won't use drugs in front of her children.

Will listen to her child, not matter what.

Always be there for her child.

Teach her children respect for elders.

Will not neglect or abandon her child.

Be independent and not depend on a man to take care of her.

Don't believe in abortions.

Show you how to have faith in God.

Make her child go to school.

Teach her daughter about boys.

Put her child first.

Let her child come back home if they mess up.

Should not give her child drugs.

A Good Father

Should be there for his child.

Teach their kids right from wrong.

Be loving and caring.

Give his kids knowledge about things.

Keep his kids from drugs.

Whip his kids.

Pay child support.

Teach his kids to respect others.

Take his kids to church.

Help his kids pick good friends.

Teach his kids how to manage money.

Teach his sons how to treat women.

Give his kids attention.

Talk to his kids.

Listen to his kids.

Show up.

Teach his kids about sex, drugs, and manners.

Teach his kids common sense.

Each one of us that have had any measure of success in life has been helped in some way by the intervention of others. The unfortunate reality is that some of these young men, though only in their teens, have been damaged rather severely. Some have sunk so deeply into their criminal mindset, they may never recover. For some, no matter what level help is offered, these young men will not make the decision to accept the help being offered to them. The harsh reality is this. All efforts will fail unless that individual can gather enough courage, desire, or inner strength to allow himself to be helped.

My Father, *this* side of Heaven

******

(An article on intervention from the NPR website, by
David Schaper, March 07, 2011)

A mentor's Goal: keeping at-risk teens alive

Albert Stinson, 38, mentors 10 boys at Marshall
High School, on Chicago's West Side. Most of them are
affiliated with gangs and have criminal records — and are
at serious risk for becoming victims of violence.

In Chicago last school year, 245 public school students
were shot, 27 of them fatally. It's a high toll. To try to find
out who might be next, Chicago Public School officials
developed a probability model by analyzing the traits of
500 shooting victims over a recent two-year period. They
noted that the vast majority were poor, black and male,
and had chronic absences, bad grades and serious
misconduct.

Using this probability model, they identified more than
200 teenagers who have a shockingly good chance of
being shot — a better than 1 in 5 chance within the next
two years.

Project Director Jonathan Moy says the probability model
isn't perfect, but it's working.

"Approximately half of the victims who have been shot this year were identified using the probability model," he says.

To reduce those awful odds, the school system is now assigning paid mentors to the teens identified to be most at risk of becoming victims of gun violence. Under the $20 million program, adult mentors counsel the teenagers in and out of school, help them find jobs and try to teach them life skills that can steer them away from violence. It's one of the most ambitious mentoring programs in the country.

Daily Fights

Albert Stinson, 38, walks through the lunchroom at his alma mater, Marshall High School on Chicago's West Side, greeting boys wearing Marshall uniforms — maroon polo shirts and khaki pants. "Hey! What's up boy? How you feeling, boy? Whatcha doing, yo?"

Stinson says he checks up on his mentees regularly."They was a part of that big gang fight last year, so I always gotta come see what's going on in the lunchroom," he says. "Sometime I wanna make sure my guys ain't into no type of squabble, or things like that".

Gangs are a big problem here: Stinson says there are fights almost every day.

Most of the 10 boys Stinson mentors at Marshall are affiliated with gangs and have criminal records. They're not in that ultra high-risk category of having a 1 in 5 chance of being shot, but they are at serious risk for becoming victims of violence.

Stinson says he's looking for signs that his boys might be agitated or angry.

"If when I go up to them and ask them how they're doing, it's a certain look," he says. "Just from being in the neighborhood, you know it. If somebody's looking a certain way, you're kind of like, 'They in more of an aggressive mode.'"

Back in the classroom that serves as the mentors' office, the solidly built Stinson says the fact that he's from this neighborhood and graduated from Marshall 20 years ago gives him credibility with the teens.

"I have the same background. I was them. And that's one thing I use to my advantage because I know what it feels to be affiliated in the court system," he says. "But I also know what it feels like to grow and that's what I'm getting them to look at when they set visionary goals — that you can grow from the dirt that's out there."

Stinson says the teenagers he works with often can't see a future. As he puts it, they "only see what's across the street," and almost everything they see is negative.

The teens NPR talked to at Marshall say it's often hard to find positive things to do and positive people to be around — and that's especially true of the men in their lives.

As someone once on the wrong path himself, Stinson says he is very aware of the lack of good role models in these boys' lives.

"I think that we do a bad job and I apologize to all of my mentees," he says. "As black men, we have failed them, because of examples we put out there."

Raw And Explosive Anger

When NPR followed Stinson at Marshall earlier this school year, he was meeting with his boys almost every day at school. Now, he focuses on visiting with them after school and at home. He goes to court with them and checks in with their probation officers and teachers. He's also trying to help them find part-time jobs.

I wanna live to see everything. My kids grow up, they kids grow up. I wanna see all that, I wanna see them graduate and go to college. I wanna see them be more than who I am.

- Antonio Fox, 17

It's the kind of attention 17-year-old Antonio Fox, one of Stinson's newest mentees, is just warming up to.

"You need a person to talk to before you do something stupid," Fox says. "You need a mentor or somebody on your side who will say something: 'Man, don't do this, don't do that.' Sometimes, you ain't gonna listen but you gotta listen so you don't get in trouble."

Antonio has been in trouble quite a bit. He was kicked out of school for fighting, but has been back since October. He's on probation and lives with an aunt because his mother "did something stupid."

But Antonio says he knows how fistfights can quickly escalate to gunbattles, and says he doesn't want to be a part of it anymore.

"I wanna live to see everything," he says. "My kids grow up, their kids grow up. I wanna see all that, I wanna see them graduate and go to college. I wanna see them be more than who I am."

But just an hour or so later, Antonio is out in the hallway, picking a fight.

"Where's my money, man!" he yells. "Where my money at, man!"

Stinson runs out to try to calm him down: "Tonio! Hey! Tonio! You don't have to be like that!"

Antonio's anger is raw and explosive — and Stinson has his hands full.

"You don't have to disrespect a brother like that, Tonio, because it's not that serious about $2, Tonio!"

No punches are thrown, but the shouting continues for more than 10 minutes, and Antonio is still furious.

I think that we do a bad job and I apologize to all of my mentees. As black men, we have failed them because of examples we put out there.

Stinson eventually calms him down and walks Antonio to class.

"You gonna be good, man?" Stinson asks. "Yeah, you smiling, man. Go into class, man!"

As he walks away, Stinson says this of Antonio: "He be all right. I trust him."

"It's basically like we've got to recondition them because they were never shown certain life skills," Stinson says. "And that's the unfortunate part because when they're not shown certain life skills, they just react. It's no critical thinking in that because they've never been shown how to sit down and try to think things through because everything is so reactionary. So you have to put in so much work and it's a process."

And officials say outside of school, significantly fewer students have been shot than at this point last year. It's not all good news though. One of the 10 boys Stinson started mentoring at Marshall back in the fall is now behind bars.

Citywide, nearly half of the kids school officials identified as being at ultra high risk for becoming victims of gun violence didn't even get into the mentoring program. Some dropped out, moved and couldn't be found; some are incarcerated; some refused to participate or their parents refused to give consent; and, yes, for a few it was too late — they'd already been shot.

******

With each young man I mentor I feel a responsibility to share with them my belief regarding each person's personal responsibility in life. I tell them all, "Regardless of the damage that has been done to you as a child, in the end it is your responsibility to take charge of your life and repair the damage. That may feel like the greatest injustice in the universe. Nevertheless, now that you are entering adulthood, you are responsible for your actions and your life. Though it may stink to the high heavens, that unfairness is simply the reality of life, this side of heaven".

Helping these young men navigate these waters is often a difficult task. It is a labor of love, hoping to help them understand that it is worth the effort to give faith and hope another chance. For this my brothers, we need all hands on deck.

At the end of the day the truth of this motto from a community organization for "at risk" males in North Carolina called BOTSO, (Brothers Organized To Serve Others), rings clear. "If we don't reach out to help save our young men, they are not at risk, we are".

Chapter 11

The Heart of the Matter

In scientific circles water is called "the source of life". It is essential for all life on earth. It is the most plentiful element in our human physical makeup. In that sense it can be considered the most important element in our makeup.

Dr. Fereydoon Batmanghelidj, M.D., is an internationally renowned researcher, author and advocate of the natural healing power of water. (See appendix for "The Water Cure") His practice in the area of medicine and healing has brought him to a dramatic conclusion. In a nutshell, he states that a large majority of health problems are directly related to that fact that humans simply do not drink enough water. High blood pressure, obesity, diabetes, asthma, joint and back pain, allergies, and many other chronic diseases are simply the body's reaction to dehydration. These ailments are just some of the examples of the body's coping mechanisms that eventually kick in when enough water is not consumed.

This speaks to the layered deception mentioned earlier. Again, it can simply be defined as reacting only to the facts that are visible on the surface, paying no attention to the unseen layers of underlying factors. When dehydration sets in it causes problem "A", and it has no immediate outward symptoms. Problem "A" causes problem "B", and it has no outward symptom. Problem "B" causes joint pain. The joint pain gets treated with pills or ointment. Meanwhile, the real source of the pain, problem A, goes untreated.

From a different point of view fathers are the source of life. Without them, none of us would be here. When fathers are missing, the resulting emotional pains of poor self-esteem, lack of direction and identity, frustration, hurt, anger, and many other symptoms flare up. Problem "A" is hurt and sadness resulting from an absentee father. That leads to problem "B", anger. Anger leads to problem C, frustration. Frustration leads to the pharmacy that sells relief in the form of drugs, illicit sex, gangs, and criminal activity, etc.

So, when society feels the pain of criminal activity, too often the only treatment is incarceration, with a patch of anger management. Society gets temporary relief, but the source of the problem festers, waiting for the next opportunity to show itself. If somehow we don't get back to treating the absentee father syndrome, we will continue to treat the symptoms and not the real problem. The solution isn't quick, but it is very simple. If we don't restore fatherhood back into our communities the curses of aimlessness, misdirection, and incarceration will completely consume our sons.

As in most major issues of life, the simplest answers are where we will find the real cure for what ails us. Physically, the solution to most of our health problems is simply to drink more water. Emotionally, we must find our way back to a culture of morality. It is the only thing that will give our children a value system with the identity and security they need. I believe that is the only way to have successful families, led by strong and loving fathers. Then we can all sit back and watch as most of the symptoms will begin to melt away.

A Bayou, a wheelchair, and a fish

Here in Houston, Texas the overall landscape is relatively flat. Drainage canals, called bayous, are used to control flooding when it rains. Some are shallow and some are rather large and deep. They can become raging rivers after heavy rains. Unless there is a long drought, many of the larger ones never go completely dry, and thus some become fishing sites.

One such bayou is next to the high school track where I often go to jog. This particular bayou, as seen in the picture above, is about 20 feet deep. It has seldom-trimmed grass, and dirt and rock-filled embankments. They can be troublesome to walk up and down by a skilled athlete. One day I noticed a man in a non-motorized wheelchair, along with his teenage son unloading fishing gear from the trunk of their car. On this particular day the grass was about knee high.

My curiosity got the best of me so I went and introduced myself. The father explained to me that this was a common fishing spot for him and his son. The father was very friendly and quickly our discussion zeroed in on the importance of fathers spending time with their sons. Much to my surprise, they were about to go down the bayou slope and go fishing!

After we talked, the two of them proceeded to work their way down the embankment. I stood there and watched in amazement as the son steadied the wheelchair from behind, and they slowly but methodically made their way down the embankment to their fishing spot. It was obvious they had done this many times before. As I watched them get to their desired spot I became more amazed when I realized that they obviously had mastered how to get back up the slope!

On my way home I was absolutely elated to see how that father understood the importance of spending quality time with his son-wheelchair and all! I can tell you with all certainty that the relationship between those two was not hampered by the father's disability, but rather strengthened by it. I could sense that the son was extremely proud and grateful to have a father who desired to spend time with him. The wheelchair, which could have been considered a hassle, became a bonding element. In recalling this event I realized an amazing truth. Just like that duo-not only do the sons need their fathers, but the fathers need their sons.

Hopefully my next book will be filled with stories similar to this one. We are in a battle for our families, fathers, and sons. We must continue to pray, teach, model, mentor, strengthen, and recapture this generation while we still can.

For many young men, restoration with their earthly father is no longer possible. However, all is not lost. There is a father in Heaven who longs to pick up the pieces. In Him there is healing for any and all hurt and anguish. In Him can be found a love, an acceptance, an identity and a significance that surpasses what even the best earthly father can provide. A loving relationship with God will provide a soothing ointment that heals completely from the inside out, with no harmful side effects.

To my young brothers I say, let the Holy Spirit to guide, and allow Jesus Christ, who is the ultimate Big Brother, to mentor you. When you do that I can assure you that in your heavenly father you will find a fullness of joy that surpasses all understanding.

I would like to leave you with this. A famous author by the name of Rudyard Kipling wrote a well-known poem called "If". In reading it I was inspired to write my own version of the poem. Between the two poems I hope you will find a word or thought to settle you and help guide you on your journey.

May God bless each and every one of you.

My Father, *this* side of Heaven

IF

(By Gregory A. Hill)

If you can take a minute

And let your heart listen to mine

If you can stop for a moment

And push the past aside

If your father is nowhere around

And confusion has clouded your way,

If it seems you're more lost than found

Just try to hear what I have to say

It wasn't God's plan to put you in dismay,

It wasn't God's plan to color your skies gray

Life has many enemies,

But you are not left to fight alone.

Somewhere there is a friend or mentor

Who can be your rock, your stone

So if your family is torn and tattered

And your hopes are in the wind,

If it seems that all that mattered

Is beyond what you can mend,

My Father, *this* side of Heaven

Don't give in just yet
To the pain and anger that is within
There is a willing hand to help you,
And it's closer than you think
If you will just hold on and reach out,
God will supply that missing link
If you make this poem your prayer
In the middle of your life's mess,
You will come to know God's plan for you-
A plan for greatness and success
If you can look beyond the hardship and pain,
You will find that they are simply part of the test
If I never get to meet you
I understand well the pain in your heart,
So just hold on
God will send you an angel
And give you a brand new start.

If
(By Rudyard Kipling)

If you can keep your head when all about you
Are losing theirs and blaming it on you;
If you can trust yourself when all men doubt you,
But make allowance for their doubting too;
If you can wait and not be tired by waiting,
Or, being lied about, don't deal in lies,
Or, being hated, don't give way to hating,
And yet don't look too good, nor talk too wise;
If you can think - and not make thoughts your aim;
If you can meet with triumph and disaster
And treat those two imposters just the same;
If you can bear to hear the truth you've spoken
Twisted by knaves to make a trap for fools,
Or watch the things you gave your life to broken,
And stoop and build 'em up with wornout tools;
If you can make one heap of all your winnings
And risk it on one turn of pitch-and-toss,
And lose, and start again at your beginnings
And never breath a word about your loss;
If you can force your heart and nerve and sinew
To serve your turn long after they are gone,
And so hold on when there is nothing in you
Except the Will which says to them: "Hold on";
If you can talk with crowds and keep your virtue,
Or walk with kings - nor lose the common touch;
If neither foes nor loving friends can hurt you;
If all men count with you, but none too much;

My Father, *this* side of Heaven

If you can fill the unforgiving minute
With sixty seconds' worth of distance run-
Yours is the Earth and everything that's in it,
And - which is more - you'll be a Man my son.

May God help us to unshackle our youth.

Appendix

Mentoring: Walking the Tight Rope

 An article form the magazine: The African Executive.

Published May 27, 2011

http://africanexecutive.com/modules/magazine/articles.php
?article=5834

"

   "...I remember extraordinary examples of mentoring during my childhood and adolescent years in Lagos Island. Here are a few of them. Just like his best friend, a young father converses with his little son as they walk home. Impressed by the tenacity and hard-work ethics of a recent high school graduate, a neighborhood landlord stops at the boy's house every other week to encourage him to seek admission into a local university. Nicknamed our "rascal" by members of his family, the naughty boy teaches his younger cousin how to construct and fly a kite, build a bird cage and design a crab trap. In a similar setting, an older kid teaches her younger friend how to boil eggs with stronger shells in saline water for the neighborhood's egg-nipping contest.

As a neighborhood "uncle" is sighted coming home from work, kids sprint towards him to help him carry his briefcase and goodies in a brown bag. Before settling down, he brings out the goodies in the bag, applies butter on each slice of bread and gives each kid one slice of bread and cake, then chats briefly with him or her about the day's school work. With absolute focus and total disregard for how long it takes, he performs this amazing routine until the last kid is attended to.

Today, the "rascal" of his family is a member of the National Assembly representing Lagos State; the older kid is an outstanding chemical engineer and a patent lawyer, now head of the patent division of maybe the largest pharmaceutical company in the US; and the neighborhood "uncle" is a retired executive of a well-known international accounting firm. Regrettably, the young father and the neighborhood landlord have passed on.

Now as an adult, I wonder if those men and women-- who dared to make a small contribution which turned out to be a significant difference in the lives of kids, teenagers and young adults--had truly inspired the next generation so positively that they are eager to pass on the baton of mentoring others like their mentors did. If not, have we who had benefited from their great generosity of time, advice, support and care allowed their remarkable efforts, which helped in preparing us for a brighter future, to die with them also?

This is a soul-searching question that we must reflect upon, individually and collectively, in order to reignite the old flame of volunteerism and mentoring for the benefit of kids, teenagers and young adults in our neighborhoods, small communities and larger societies.

The positive results of mentoring are clearly evident. All over the world, beneficiaries of mentoring are often highly successful and respected individuals with representation from every race, ethnicity, religion, gender and profession. Everyday, professionals who mentor and are mentored include doctors, nurses, teachers, accountants, lawyers, revered religious leaders, presidents, vice presidents, state governors, members of the legislative and judicial branches of government, professors, mathematicians, statisticians, business tycoons, school administrators, engineers, pilots, and even generals in the Army, Navy, Air Force and Marine.

Indubitably, mentors leave powerful imprints in our lives during our childhood and adolescence, and that these imprints tend to remain fresh in our memories far into our adult years. Either consciously or subconsciously, we tend to return or give back similar favors to our old communities or introduce similar initiatives to our new communities, including our extended families, neighborhoods, communities, societies, workplaces, old schools and universities.

The negative results of mentoring are clearly evident also. Some mentors-- especially those with a tendency to abuse power--abuse kids, teenagers and young adults whom they mentor. Their charisma, position of authority and larger-than-life impressions tend to create an aura or appearance that is appealing and captivating to inexperienced, young and gullible souls. For example, decades of sexual abuse of minors by Catholic priests who were once regarded as mentors with high moral values and divine calling, is an unimpressive outcome of mentoring. How could their victims challenge such respected men with close-to-divine status or who deliver divine interpretations to them? To whom would the victims lodge their complaints? To the parents who tell their kids that the clergy can do no wrong? To the top hierarchy of the Church who deliberately concealed and took unusually long time to admit to such violations by priests under their charge? Only recently did the top hierarchy of the Church regret its late admission of such abuses and promised to allow accused priests to be prosecuted for crimes against minors in the jurisdiction where they were committed.

Regardless of either outcome, mentors provide the following services to their students: guidance, protection, parenting, nurturing, coaching, advisory, counseling, emotional and financial support, and consulting. Mentors demonstrate the capacities to listen attentively, to observe human conditions from different perspectives, to impart knowledge, to tell stories of their experiences at the right moments and in relevant ways, to exercise a lot of patience, to correct erring behaviors of their students, to do some hand-holding when necessary, to comfort and reassure their students at times of uncertainty and disillusionment, to recognize when change is necessary and must be made, and to build confidence in their students one day at a time. Without a cue from someone else, mentors transition seamlessly into different roles at the right time as a guide, guardian, nurturer, coach, teacher, consultant, counsel, confidence-builder, substitute parent, supporter, friend, and occasionally an antagonist of bad behavior.

As a result, beneficiaries of proper mentoring are likely to have an early preview of a world with numerous possibilities and make less common mistakes than their contemporaries. Besides, the great hidden qualities of mentored individuals are likely to be unveiled and sharpened early; habits which would have hindered their future are likely to be corrected early; and mentored individuals are likely to be encouraged to focus on the fields where they show the greatest strength or potential. With unrestricted access to the mentor and open line of communication between mentor and the mentored, exchange of ideas and views is likely to be as fruitful as a fruit tree growing at the edge of a stream; and such an uninhibited exchange of ideas is likely to benefit the protégé immensely, particularly in a learning environment or professional setting. And lucky are mentored individuals who get early exposure to the right people who are strongly committed to making a difference in the lives of others or are experts in their fields; and who gain long-term friendship with their mentors.

Now we need quiet volunteers to bring back mentoring into our urban neighborhoods in spite of our urbane way of living or lifestyle, and into our rural communities. We need men and women who dare to make a difference in the lives of kids, teenagers and young adults, without dampening their spirit of hope, abusing or dehumanizing them. We need men and women who can quietly impart knowledge through exposure of their students to practical and intellectual discourse; visitations to historical sites, culturally notable sites, zoos, safaris, museums, classical concerts and local theatres; involvement of their students in sports, theatre, dance, ballet and leadership training; and myriads of other activities for our youths. Who else can make this dream come true? Besides individual volunteers, groups such as socially responsible corporations, non-governmental organizations (NGOs), advocates of volunteerism and mentoring, and religious organizations can contribute tremendously to mentoring.

Concerned parents just need to watch out for the tell-tale signs of abuse of their minors, such as withdrawal, unusual mood swings, deliberate avoidance of the mentor in speech or when sighted, and hostility toward a mentor once held in utter admiration.

Then, we can experience once again the tremendous joy in being mentors of our nation's future leaders: the kids, teenagers and young adults in our neighborhoods, schools, and communities, as well as at our places of worship and playgrounds. Their bright future depends on how we mentor them today. So, let's get started!"

The Water Cure

(Below is a portion of the main article. A link is provided at the end to examine the rest of the story).

Discovery of the water cure

Mike: Welcome everyone, this is Mike Adams with Truth Publishing, and today I'm very excited to be welcoming Dr. Batmanghelidj, author of Water For Health, For Healing, For Life. Welcome, Dr. Batmanghelidj.

Dr. B: Thank you very much for inviting me to be on the air with you and giving me the opportunity of sharing my thoughts on the future of medicine in this country.

Mike: I think there are many, many people who have read your books. People are intrigued by the idea that water can be a therapy, a healing substance for the human body. What is it about water? How did you first become aware of these healing properties of water?

Dr. B: Well, it's very bizarre. As you know, I'm a regular doctor, an M.D. I had the honor and the privilege of being selected as one of the house doctors, and I had the extreme honor of being one of the last students of Sir Alexander Fleming, the discoverer of penicillin. I mention his name so that you know I was immersed in medical school and research. And some years later, I had to give two glasses of water to a person who was doubled up in abdominal pain from his disease, because I had no other medication to give him at that moment. And he was in excruciating pain, and water performed miraculous relief for him. It gave him relief -- within three minutes his pain diminished, and within eight minutes it disappeared completely, whereas he was doubled up eight minutes before and he couldn't even walk, he completely recovered from that situation. And he started beaming from ear to ear, very happy, asked me what happens if the pain comes back? I said, "Well, drink more water." Then I decided to instruct him to drink two glasses of water every three hours. Which he did, and that was the end of his ulcer pains for the rest of the duration that he was with me.

Mike: And from that episode then, what happened next?

Dr. B: That woke me up, because in medical school I'd never heard that water could cure pain, that kind of pain, in fact. And so I had the occasion to test water as a medication in subsequently over 3,000 similar cases. And water proved every time to be an effective medication. I came away from that experience with the understanding that these people were all thirsty, and that thirst in the body can manifest itself in the form of abdominal pain to the level that the person can even become semi-conscious, because that's the experience I had. And water picks them up every time.

So when I came to America in 1982, I went to the University of Pennsylvania, where I was invited to continue my research, and did research in the pain-relieving properties of water. I asked myself, why does the pharmaceutical industry insist on using antihistamines for this kind of pain medication? So I started researching the role of histamine in the body, and the answer was there -- histamine is a neurotransmitter in charge of water regulation and the drought management programs of the body. When it manifests pain, in fact, it is indicating dehydration.

So, the body does manifest dehydration in the form of pain. Now, depending on where dehydration is settled, you feel pain there. Very simple, and I presented this concept at the international conference as the guest lecturer of a conference on cancer, explaining that the human body manifests dehydration by producing pain, and pain is a sign of water shortage in the body, and water shortage is actually the background to most of the health problems in our society.

Because if you look at what the pharmaceutical industry is doing, they're producing so many different antihistamines as medication. Antidepressant drugs are antihistamines, pain medication are antihistamines, other medications are directly and indirectly antihistamines. So, that is when my work was published, the scientific secretariat of the 3rd Interscience Board Conference of Inflammation invited me to make this presentation on histamine at their conference in 1989, in Monte Carlo. And I did that, and so it became a regular understanding that histamine is a water regulator in the body. But unfortunately, this information is not reaching the public through the medical community because it's not a money-maker.

So that's when I began to consider writing for the public, so that the public could become aware of the problem directly without the interference of a doctor, and that's how I have generated all my medical information for the public. Of course, I have published extensively for the scientific community, but no one is picking up. In fact, the NIH, the Office of Alternative Medicine, had its first conference when the office was created, and I was asked to make my presentation, but when the proceedings of the conference came out, my presentation was censored after the proceedings. So there is a movement afoot within the NIH group of people to keep a closed lid on my information so that it doesn't get out, because obviously they are more in favor of the drug industry, because it is now obvious that they are getting paid by them.

Mike: I think it is, first of all, that is an amazing account of what has been happening, and I think it is fair to say, too, that the pharmaceutical industry and organized medicine in general, really doesn't want to promote anything that is free or near-free to the average patient. Sunlight is available at no charge, water is available at nearly no charge -- would you agree that their thinking is if people can cure their diseases, and achieve a high state of health on their own with these free substances, then that diminishes their profits and their importance?

Dr. B: Absolutely. That's why I've created an organization now called National Association for Honesty in Medicine. Because I think it's totally dishonest, in fact, criminal, to treat a person who is just thirsty, and give them toxic medication so that he gets sick and dies earlier than normal.

Mike: Can you give out the web address to that organization, by the way?

Dr. B: My website is http://www.watercure.com -- it gives you the option of going to one site or the other -- either Water Cure.com, or you can go the National Association for Honesty in Medicine. Or you can go to the information side of my website, http://www.watercure.com, because I have posted all of my scientific articles on dehydration on the website, and lots of other free information that people can have.
Learn more:
http://www.naturalnews.com/Report_water_cure_1.html#ixzz1 tismWRmI

I welcome your comments and concerns, and they can be shared on the following email address: gahpublishing@yahoo.com. (Please put the book title in the subject line).

My Father, *this* side of Heaven